Bond

No.1 for exam success

Maths

10 Minute Tests

10-11+ years

OXFORD
UNIVERSITY PRESS

Test 1: **Shape and Space**

Test time: 0 5 10 minutes

1

What fraction of 2 hours is 15 minutes?
Circle the answer.

$\frac{1}{4}$ $\frac{1}{2}$ $\frac{2}{15}$ $\frac{1}{8}$ $\frac{1}{3}$

2

A 24-hour digital clock shows:

What would the time be if it were shown on a 12-hour clock?
Circle the answer.

A 9.42 **B** 9.42 am **C** 9.42 pm
D 12.42 pm **E** 8.42 pm

3

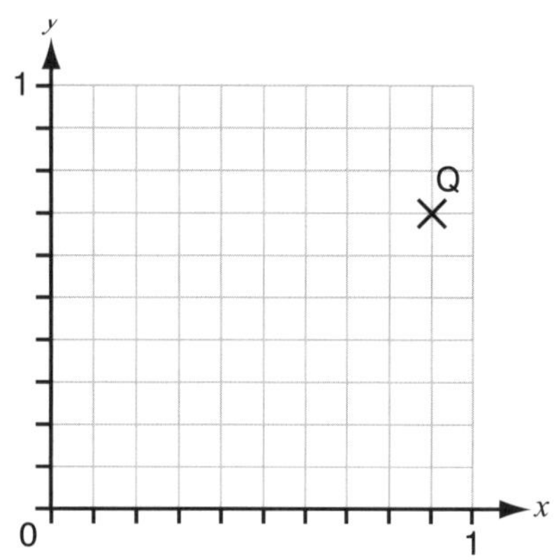

What are the coordinates of Q?
Circle the answer.

A (0.7, 0.9) **B** (0.9, 0.7) **C** (1.9, 0.7)
D (1.7, 0.9) **E** (0.5, 0.6)

4

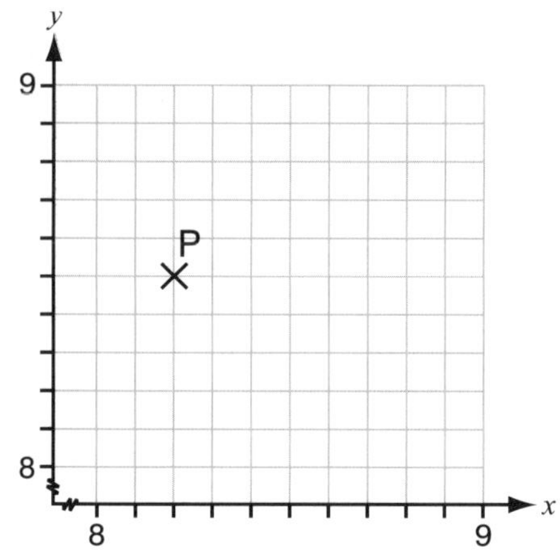

Using the grid, write down the coordinates of P.

____

5

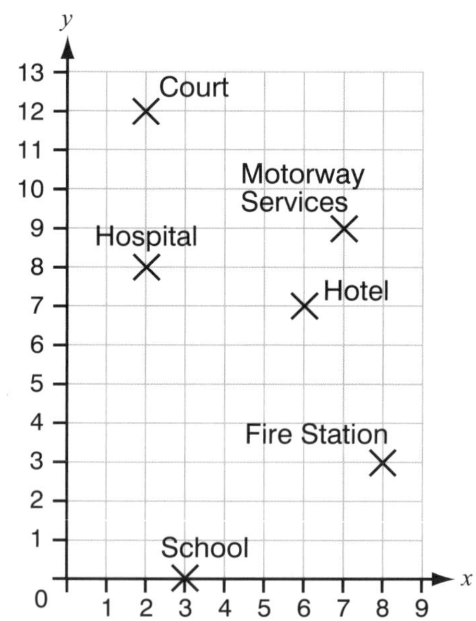

Where is the hotel?

____

6

Give the coordinates of the train station.

(______ , ______)

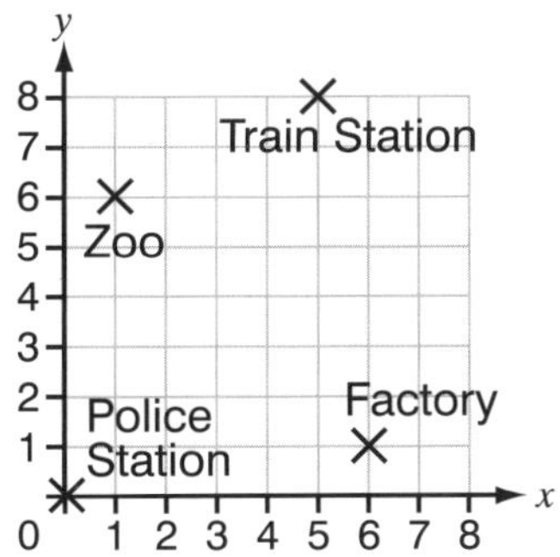

7

Which of the following options correctly lists the coordinates of all three points?

Circle the answer.

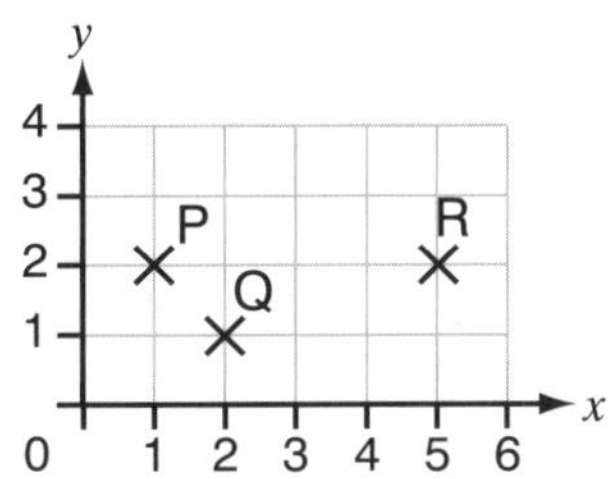

A P(1, 2) Q(2, 1) R(5, 2)

B P(2, 1) Q(1, 2) R(2, 5)

C P(1, 2) Q(1, 2) R(5, 2)

D P(2, 1) Q(2, 1) R(5, 2)

E P(1, 2) Q(2, 1) R(2, 5)

8

What are the coordinates of the points R, S and T?

Circle the answer.

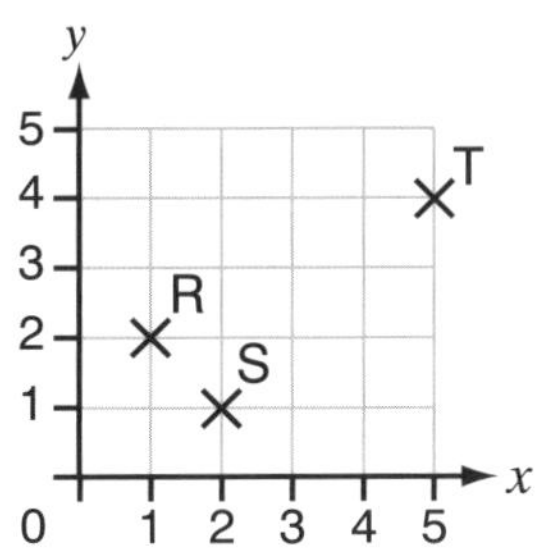

A R(1, 2) S(2, 1) T(4, 5)

B R(2, 1) S(1, 2) T(4, 5)

C R(1, 2) S(2, 1) T(5, 4)

D R(1, 1) S(2, 1) T(4, 5)

E R(1, 2) S(1, 2) T(5, 4)

9

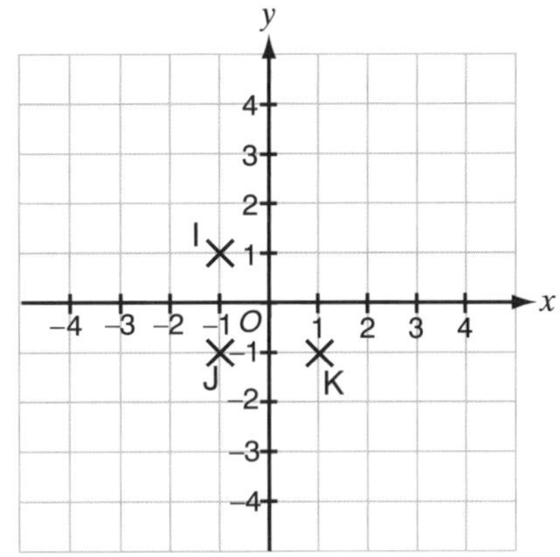

What are the coordinates of the points I, J and K?

Circle the answer.

A I(–1, 1) J(1, 1) K(1, –1)

B I(1, –1) J(–1, –1) K(–1, 1)

C I(–1, 1) J(–1, –1) K(–1, 1)

D I(1, –1) J(–1, –1) K(1, –1)

E I(–1, 1) J(–1, –1) K(1, –1)

10

A, B and D form three corners of a square.

What are the coordinates of point C, which completes the square?

Circle the answer.

(2, –2) **(–2, 2)** **(–2, –2)** **(2, 2)** **(2, 0)**

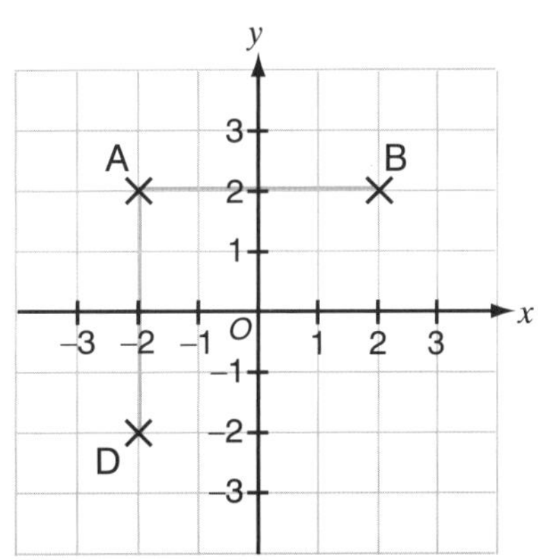

Total

Test 2: Number

Test time: 0 5 10 minutes

1 What is the number 59 038 in words? Circle the answer.

A Fifty-nine thousand and thirty-eight

B Five hundred and ninety thousand and thirty-eight

C Fifty-nine thousand three hundred and eighty

D Five thousand nine hundred and thirty-eight

E Five hundred and nine thousand and thirty-eight

2 Ninety thousand nine hundred and nine.

Which answer shows this written as a number?

Circle the answer.

99 099 99 999 90 909
90 009 90 099

3 103 247

The 2 in this number is worth two hundred.

What is the three worth?

Circle the answer.

A Three hundred **B** Thirty

C Three **D** Thirty thousand

E Three thousand

4

Find a number for the blank space so that the list is in order of size.

2.35, 2.39, ……, 2.42

Circle the answer.

A 2.40 **B** 2.3 **C** 2.421

D 2.381 **E** 2.30

5

13, 130, ……, 13 000, 130 000

What should be the value of the 3 in the missing term?

____

6 From the list find the smallest number. Circle the answer.

7.6 7.06 7.60 7.006 7.600

7

In a class of 30 pupils, 11 are girls.

Approximately what proportion are boys?

Circle the most appropriate answer.

$\frac{1}{2}$ $\frac{11}{30}$ $\frac{1}{3}$ $\frac{2}{3}$ $\frac{5}{6}$

8

To make 2500 ml of orange squash, 500 ml of concentrate must be used.

What proportion of water must be used to make up the rest?

Circle the answer.

$\frac{1}{5}$ $\frac{1}{4}$ $\frac{4}{5}$ $\frac{3}{4}$ $\frac{2}{5}$

9 7.6324

What is this number to two decimal places?

____

10 8.9956

What is this number to two decimal places?

Circle the answer.

9.00 8.99 8.90 9.0000 9.0056

Total

Test 3: **Shape and Space**

Test time: 0 5 10 minutes

1

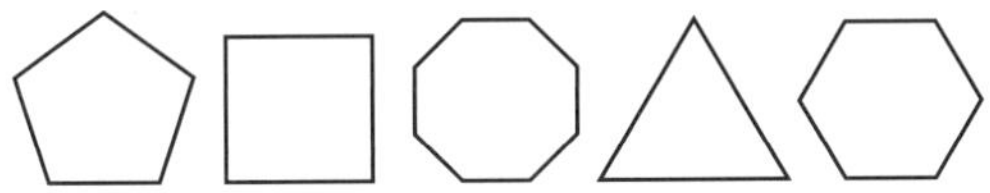

A **B** **C** **D** **E**

An angle inside a polygon is called an interior angle.

Which of the above polygons has the smallest interior angle?

Circle the answer.

2

Which of the following shapes has nine diagonals?

Circle the answer.

A Pentagon **B** Quadrilateral **C** Octagon

D Triangle **E** Hexagon

3

Which of these makes a word when rotated through 180°?

Circle the answer.

SIH **ISH** **HIS** **SHI** **IHS**

4

A **B** **C** **D** **E**

Which of these shapes has rotational symmetry?

Circle the answer.

5

Which of these does not have a vertical line of symmetry?

Circle the answer.

MUM **TAT** **HAH** **LAL** **XOX**

6

Which of these has a horizontal line of symmetry?

Circle the answer.

DID **CAT** **HUH** **NUN** **TAT**

7-8

What is the perimeter of each of the shapes below?

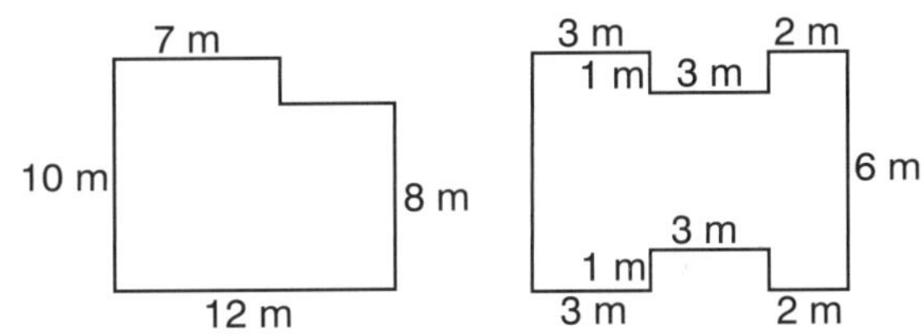

_____________ m _____________ m

9

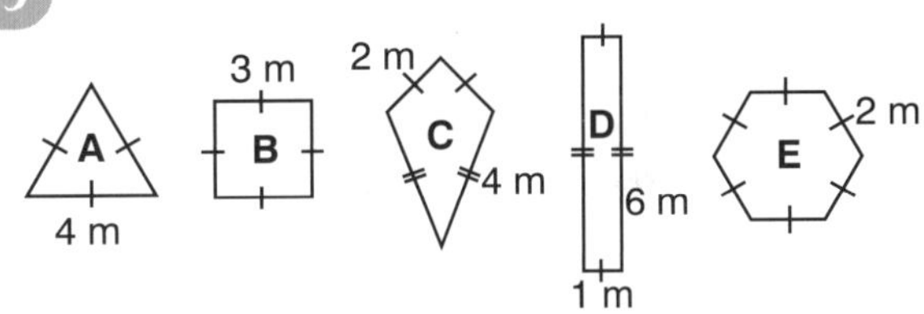

Which shape has a different perimeter from the others?

____

10

What is the perimeter of this shape?

Circle the answer.

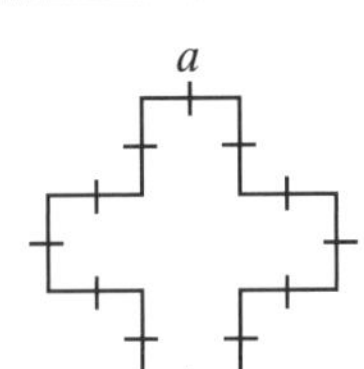

A $12a$ **B** a^{12} **C** $6a$

D $aaaaaa$ **E** a^6

Total

TEST 4: Data Handling

1

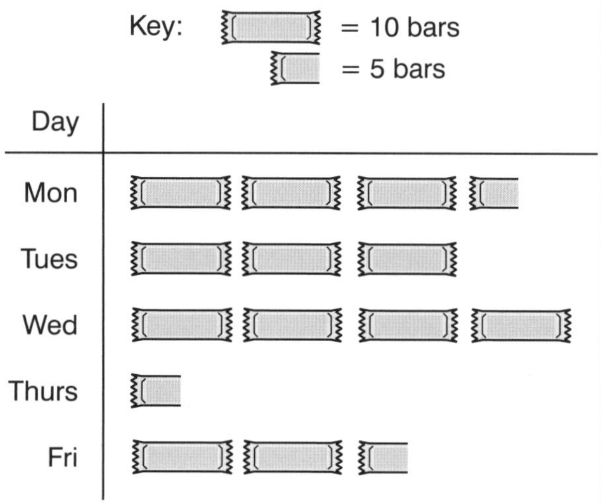

How many fruit bars were sold on Wednesday?

____

2

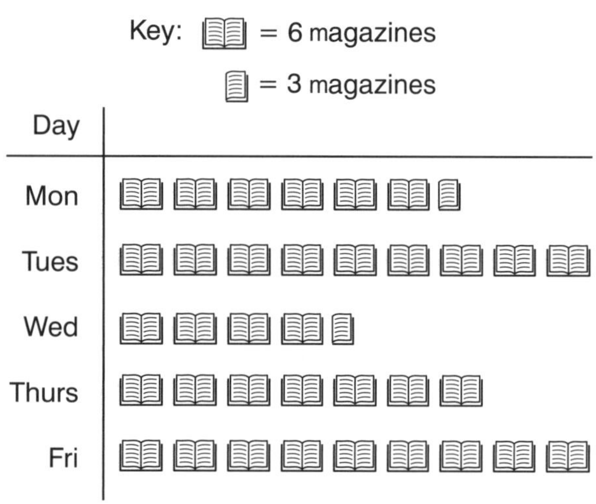

How many more magazines were sold on Monday than on Wednesday?

Circle the answer.

A 12 **B** Can't tell **C** 2

D $6\frac{1}{2}$ **E** 0

3

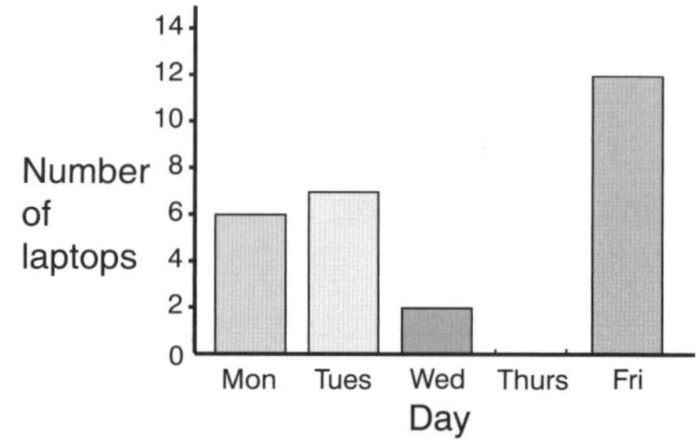

How many more laptops were bought on Friday than on Tuesday?

____

4

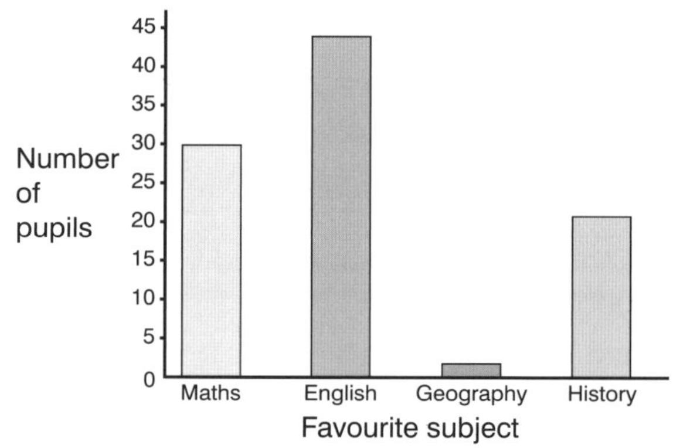

How many more pupils prefer maths than geography?

____

5

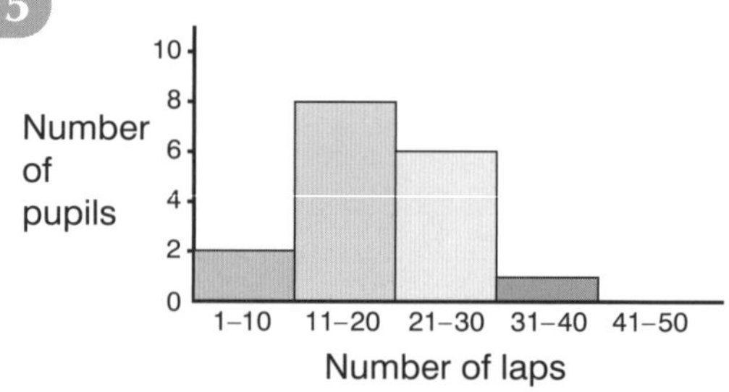

How many pupils completed more than 20 laps in a charity race?

____

6

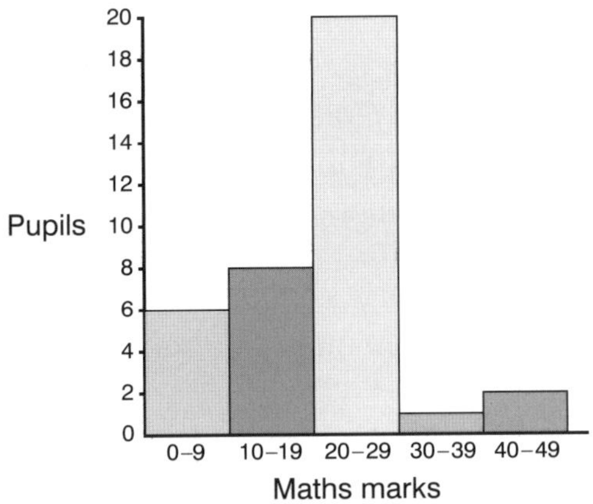

The pass mark for a maths test was 20.

How many pupils passed the test?

____

7

A bag contains 2 red, 4 green and 6 yellow marbles. Lily picks a marble at random.

In which of the options below are both statements true? Circle the answer.

A You have an even chance of picking a yellow marble.
You have a greater than even chance of picking a red marble.

B You are certain to pick a marble.
You have a greater than even chance of picking a yellow marble.

C You have a less than even chance of picking a red marble.
You have a less than even chance of picking a green marble.

D You have a greater than even chance of picking a yellow marble.
You have a less than even chance of picking a green marble.

E You have a greater than even chance of picking a green marble.
You have an even chance of picking a yellow marble.

8

Jo rolls a fair dice numbered 1 to 6. In which of the options below are both statements true?

Circle the answer.

A You have an even chance of rolling an even number.
You are certain to roll a number less than six.

B You have an even chance of rolling a prime number.
You are certain to roll a number less than seven.

C You have a less than even chance of rolling an odd number.
You are certain to roll a number less than seven.

D You have a greater than even chance of rolling a prime number.
You are certain to roll a number less than five.

E You have a less than even chance of rolling a prime number.
You have an even chance of rolling an odd number.

9

A bag contains some coloured balls.

There are: 3 black, 2 red, 5 blue, 6 green and 7 yellow.

Ranjna picks a ball at random.

What is the chance that she doesn't pick a red ball?

____

10

When Eric spins the spinner, what is the probability that it will land on a number greater than 1?

____

Total

TEST 5: **Number**

Test time: 0 5 10 minutes

1 1 8 9 15 16

Look at these numbers. Which is neither a square number nor a cube number?

Circle the answer.

2 1 2 9 16 25

Look at these numbers. Which is both a square number and a cube number?

Circle the answer.

3

Which option shows two prime numbers that add up to make a cube number?

Circle the letter.

A 3 and 5 **B** 1 and 7 **C** 2 and 6

D 5 and 120 **E** 4 and 12

4

Look at the pattern below:

Line 1	1 = 1
Line 2	1 + 3 = 4
Line 3	1 + 3 + 5 = 9
Line 4	1 + 3 + 5 + 7 = 16
Line 5	1 + 3 + 5 + 7 + 9 = 25

How many prime numbers would line 6 contain?

____

5

Out of 567 people surveyed, 78 preferred curries, 206 preferred stir-fries and the rest preferred pasta.

How many liked pasta?

____

6

127 children from Grassmoor Primary School are performing a show.

72 children are acting, 49 children are assisting backstage. The rest are helping in the front of house.

How many are helping in the front of house?

____

7-8

The caterers at a concert make 728 meals.

Unfortunately 986 people turn up.

How many people go without a meal?

____

If an extra 300 meals are made, how many are left over?

____

9

A bus starts at the terminus. It stops three times before it reaches the airport.

35 people get on at the terminus.

14 people get on at the school, 2 get off.

12 get on at the hospital and 16 get off.

6 get on in the High St and 28 get off.

How many people are on the bus when it arrives at the airport?

____

10

Sara buys some clothes worth £58.63.

As she spends over £50 she receives a £5 discount.

How much does she pay in total?

____

Total

TEST 6: Data Handling

Test time: 0 5 10 minutes

1

25	27	26	27	25	24	25
24	26	27	28	30	30	27

The midday temperatures in °C recorded over a fortnight are shown above.

What is the mode?

__________ °C

2

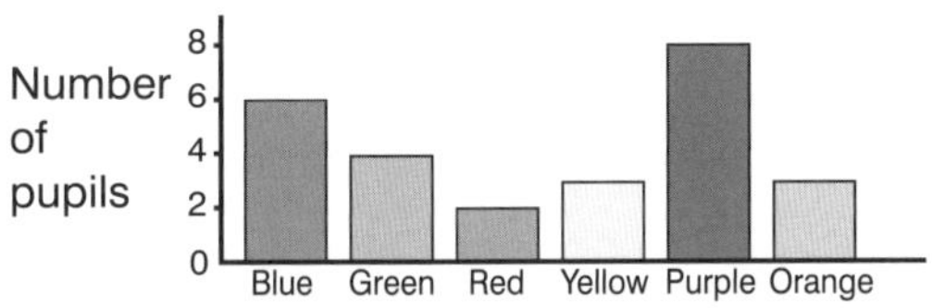

This graph shows the favourite colours of Year 5.

What is the modal colour?

____

3 Seven people's wages are listed below.

£110 £150 £120 £130 £140 £220 £435

What is the median wage?

Circle the answer.

A £143 **B** £435 **C** £186

D £140 **E** £130

4 The total attendance in one season for Cliffridge Football Club was 960 000.

They played 24 games.

What was the mean attendance?

____

5

Month	May	June	July	Aug	Sep
Hours	174	186	191	199	188

Find the range for the hours of sunshine shown in the table above.

Circle the answer.

A 26 **B** 199 **C** 186 **D** 5 **E** 25

6 6 4 2 0 8

Find the range of the numbers above.

Circle the answer.

A 8 **B** 0 **C** 4 **D** 6 **E** 20

7 8 6 2 1 13

Find the range of the numbers above.

Circle the answer.

A 13 **B** 1 **C** 12 **D** 8 **E** 30

8 12 7 20 5 19

What is the median of these numbers?

Circle the answer.

A 20 **B** 12 **C** 62 **D** 7 **E** 19

9

Day	Mon	Tues	Wed	Thurs	Fri
No. of cups	2		8	9	4

Heather thinks her mum is drinking too many cups of coffee a day.

Heather asks her some questions and completes this table.

Her mum says her mean is 7.

How many cups did she drink on Tuesday?

____

10

Day	Mon	Tues	Wed	Thurs	Fri
Hours	12	13	8		4

Ali's dad thinks Ali is spending too many hours playing games on the computer.

His dad asks Ali some questions and completes this table.

Ali's dad says his mean is 9.

How many hours did Ali play games on Thursday?

____

Time for a break! Go to Puzzle Page 42

Total

Test time: 0 5 10 minutes

TEST 7: Shape and Space

1

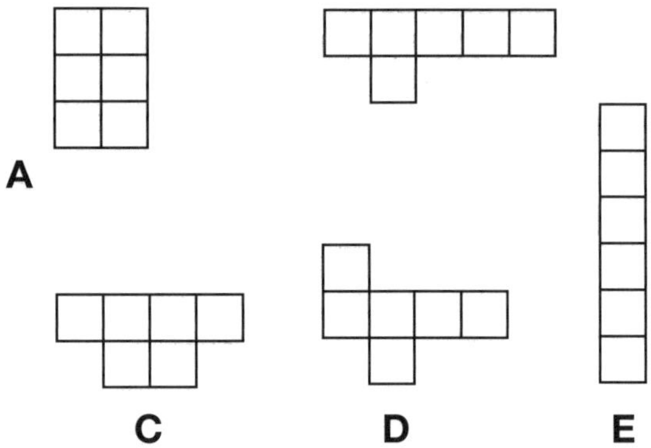

Look at the nets above.
Which one is the net of a closed cube?
Circle the answer.

2

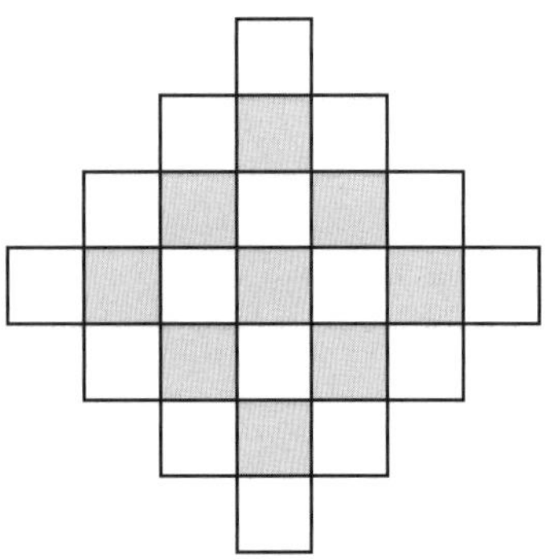

All squares measure 30 cm by 30 cm.
What is the area of the entire pattern in m^2?
Circle the answer.

A 25.2 m^2

B 2.52 m^2

C 2520 m^2

D 2.25 m^2

E 22 500 m^2

3

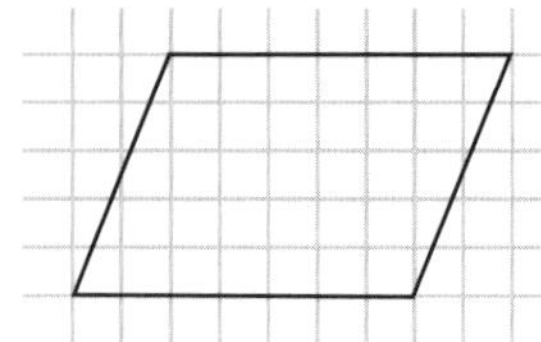

In the diagram above 1 square represents 1 cm^2.
What is the area of the parallelogram?

________ cm^2

4

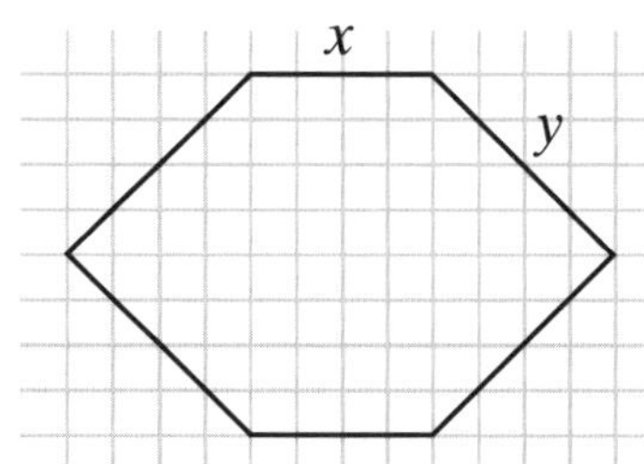

What is the correct formula for the area of this shape?
Circle the answer.

A $4x^2$ **B** $(x + y)^2$

C $2x^2y^2$ **D** $\frac{1}{2}xy$

E $2x^2 + 2y^2$

5

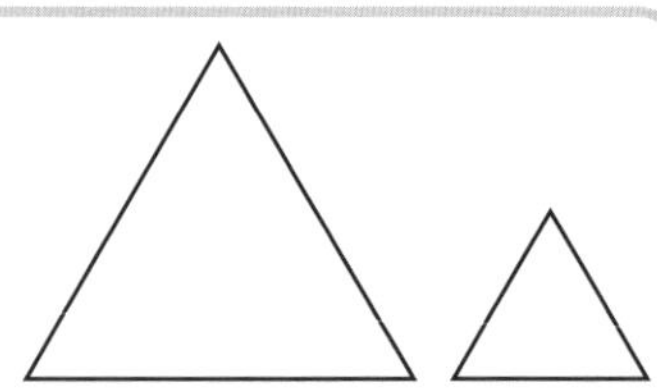

The side length of the smaller equilateral triangle is half the side length of the larger equilateral triangle.
How many times will the smaller triangle fit into the larger triangle?
Circle the answer.

2 3 4 5 6

6

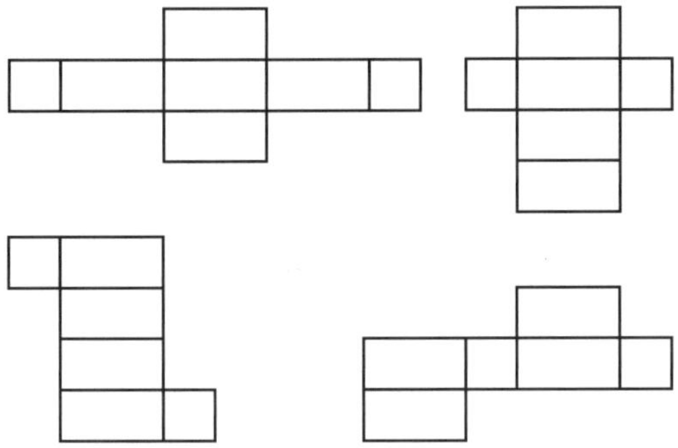

How many of the nets shown above will form a closed cuboid when folded?

Circle the answer.

A None of them

B Only 1 of them

C 2 of them

D 3 of them

E All of them

7

What is the area of the triangle shown?

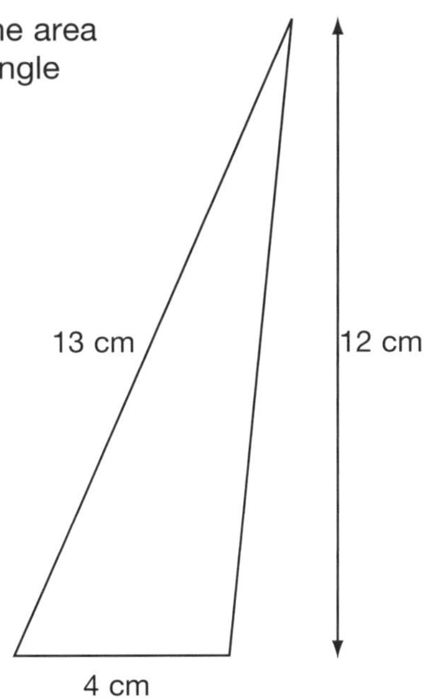

__________ cm^2

8

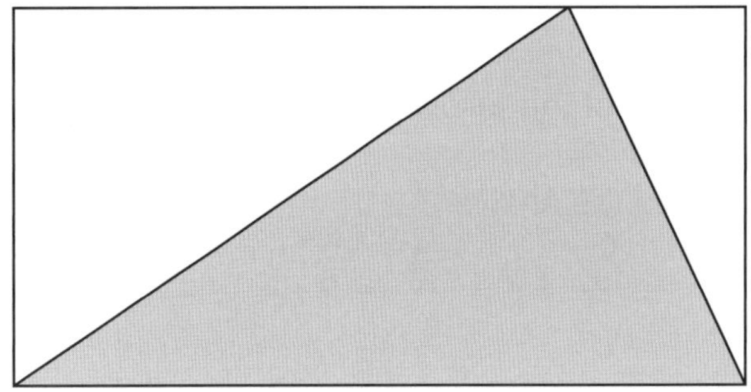

The area of the rectangle is 15 cm^2.

What is the area of the triangle?

__________ cm^2

9

The area of a rectangle is 70 cm^2.

What could be the perimeter of the rectangle?

Circle the answer.

A 7 cm

B 9 cm

C 12 cm

D 26 cm

E 34 cm

10

The perimeter of a rectangle is 24 cm.

If the rectangle is 10 cm long, what is the area of the rectangle?

Circle the answer.

A 10 cm^2

B 11 cm^2

C 20 cm^2

D 32 cm^2

E 220 cm^2

Total

Test 8: Number

Test time: 0 5 10 minutes

1

Which of the following has the smallest value?

Circle the answer.

$\frac{1}{2}$ $\frac{6}{10}$ $\frac{3}{5}$ $\frac{4}{9}$ $\frac{5}{8}$

2

Which of the following has the largest value?

Circle the answer.

$\frac{2}{5}$ 20% $\frac{1}{3}$ 35% 0.3

3

Which option is different from the others?

Circle the answer.

A $\frac{3}{4}$ of 200 **B** 75% of 200

C 0.75 of 200 **D** 0.5 of 400

E 150% of 100

4

Which option has the largest value?

Circle the answer.

A 62% of 60 **B** 0.63 of 60 **C** $\frac{3}{5}$ of 60

D $\frac{2}{3}$ of 60 **E** $\frac{5}{8}$ of 60

5

Jane scores 17 out of 25 in a maths test.

What percentage did she get?

____

6

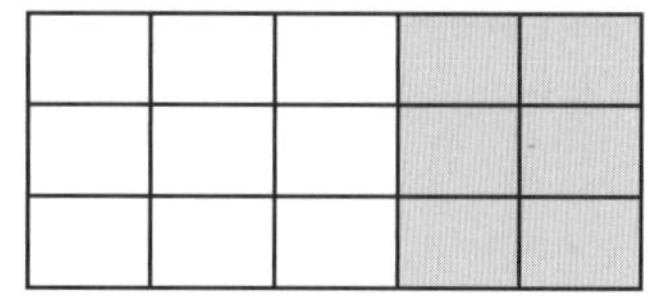

What percentage of the diagram is shaded?

____

7

Rowan has 50 marbles.

He gives 13 to Jack and keeps the rest.

What percentage does he keep for himself?

____

8

Ajay noticed that out of 400 buildings, 20% of them were terraced houses.

How many terraced houses are there?

____

9

A sofa costs £1800.

During a sale the price is reduced by a third.

What is the sale price of the sofa?

____

10

Out of 1400 dog owners surveyed, 8 out of 10 bought 'Doggy' dog food.

How many people bought other brands?

____

Total

Test 9: **Shape and Space**

Test time:

1-2

Below are 2 nets of open cuboids.

When each net is folded, it makes an open box.

What is the volume of each box?

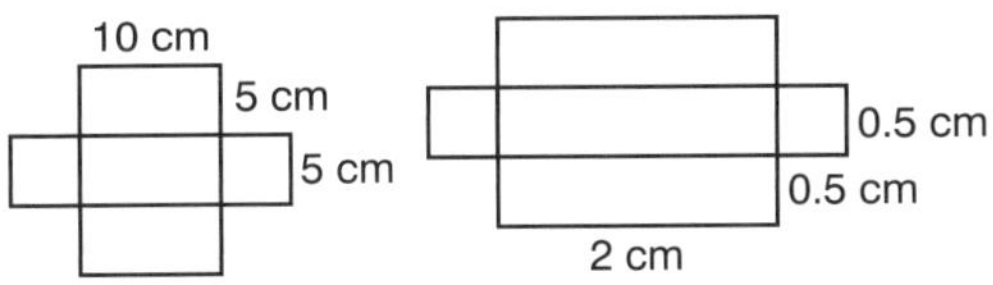

____________ cm^3 ____________ cm^3

3

What number does the arrow point to in the scale?

____

4

Tom buys three 2 litre bottles of water, 1.5 litres of milk and a 1 kg bag of potatoes.

What is the total weight of the shopping?

Circle the answer.

A 0.5 kg **B** 2.5 kg **C** 5.5 kg

D 8.5 kg **E** 10.5 kg

5

The weight limit for airline luggage is 25 kg.

A case weighs 25.80 kg.

An item weighing 850 g is removed.

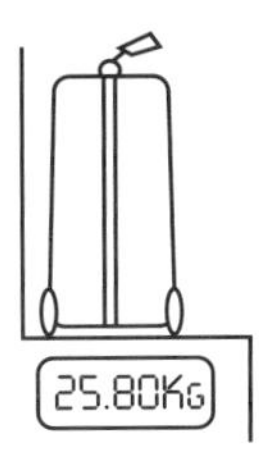

How much does the case now weigh?

Circle the answer.

A 24.95 kg **B** 26.65 kg **C** 25.95 kg

D –825.80 kg **E** 17.30 kg

6

A tree is about 6 times the height of a tall man who is standing next to it.

Circle the answer that would be the closest to the height of the tree.

A 50 m **B** 2000 mm **C** 40 cm

D 5 mm **E** 12 m

7

Tim buys a medium-sized rucksack.

Approximately how many litres will it hold?

Circle the answer.

A 0.5 litres **B** 5 litres **C** 50 litres

D 500 litres **E** 5000 litres

8

Which container will hold about 20 litres?

Circle the correct letter.

A a bath **B** a sink **C** a kettle

D a milk bottle **E** an egg cup

9

What is the area of this shape?

__________ m^2

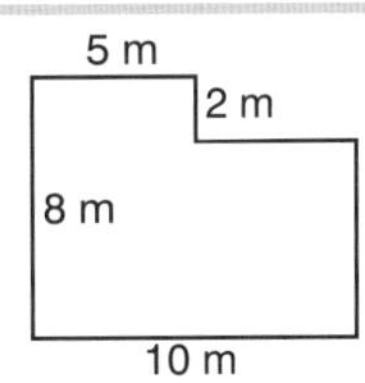

10

The area of the shaded triangle is 1000 mm^2.

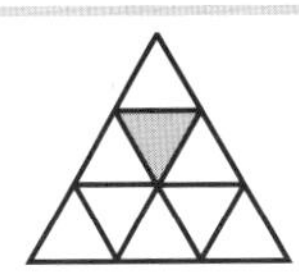

What is the area of the larger triangle?

Circle the answer.

A 90000 mm^2 **B** 8000 mm^2 **C** 9.0 cm^2

D 90 cm^2 **E** 900 cm^2

Total

TEST 10: **Number**

Test time: 0 5 10 minutes

1

Out of 24 pairs of jeans, $\frac{2}{3}$ of them are blue.

How many pairs of jeans are blue?

____

2

300 people are surveyed.

$\frac{2}{5}$ of them are 21 and under.

How many are 21 and under?

____

3

250 people visit a coffee shop.

$\frac{3}{10}$ of the people order black coffee.

The rest order white coffee.

How many people order white coffee?

____

4

200 flights leave Abbeytown airport in one day.

$\frac{4}{5}$ are domestic and the rest are international.

How many flights are international?

____

5

In a 26-mile marathon, Gary sprints $\frac{1}{13}$ of the way, jogs $\frac{7}{13}$ of the way and walks the rest of the way.

How many miles does he walk for?

_______ miles

6

The journey time from Greentown to Greenberg normally takes 40 minutes.

Due to traffic congestion, journey times have increased by 15%.

What is the new journey time?

____

7

Asima has £64.

She gives $\frac{1}{8}$ to Mary.

She gives $\frac{3}{8}$ to Jason.

The rest is given to Nabeel.

How much is Nabeel given?

____

8

A shirt costs £30 before a '20% off everything' sale.

How much is the shirt in the sale?

____

9

500 ml out of a 2.5 litre bottle of orange squash is concentrate.

What fraction is concentrate?

Circle the answer.

$\frac{1}{5}$ $\frac{1}{4}$ $\frac{1}{3}$ $\frac{1}{2}$ $\frac{1}{25}$

10

4 kg of a certain type of food contains 20 g of fat.

What fraction of the food is fat?

____

Total

TEST 11: **Algebra**

Test time: 0 5 10 minutes

1

I think of a number and multiply it by 4, then add 12. The answer I get is 76.

What number did I think of?

____

2

Gary has 21 marbles.

He has x red marbles.

He has three more blue marbles than red.

He has four times as many green as red.

How many red marbles does he have?

____

3

The numbers 1, 2, and 3 are consecutive.

Their sum is $1 + 2 + 3 = 6$.

The sum of another set of three consecutive whole numbers is 21.

Find the smallest of these numbers.

____

4

Linda has £3.60 and Mike has £4.80.

Mike gives Linda some 20p coins.

They then have the same amount of money.

How many 20p coins did Mike give Linda?

____

5

$5x + 3y = 2z$

Find the value of z when $x = 5$ and $y = 3$.

____

6

Akshay was x years old 5 years ago.

How old will he be in 7 years time?

Circle the answer.

A $x + 2$ **B** $x - 12$ **C** $12 - x$

D $12 + x$ **E** $x + 7$

7

y is $\frac{4}{5}$ of x.

Look at the list of statements below.

Circle the statement which is incorrect.

A $y = \frac{4}{5}x$ **B** $x = \frac{5}{4}y$ **C** $5y = 4x$

D $4y = 5x$ **E** $\frac{y}{x} = \frac{4}{5}$

8

A rectangle has a width x cm.

Its length is twice as long as its width.

Find an expression for the perimeter of the rectangle in terms of x.

____

9

Minibuses have x seats. Coaches have y seats.

Bruce hires 2 minibuses and 7 coaches.

How many seats will there be in total?

Leave your answer in terms of x and y.

____

10

If $7x - 9 = 10x - 18$, what is the value of x?

____

Total

TEST 12: **Data Handling**

Test time: 0 5 10 minutes

1

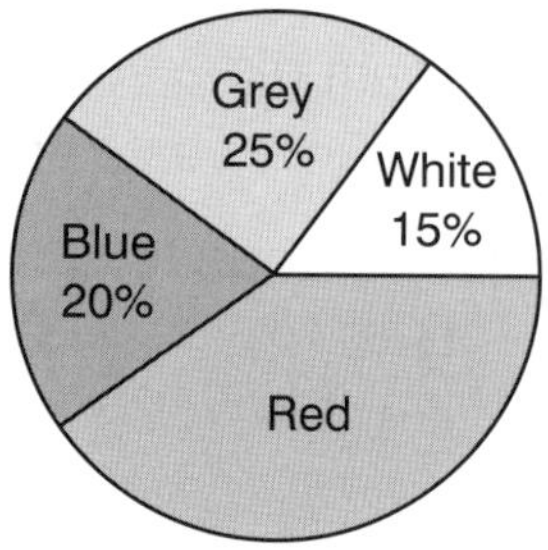

The are 700 cars in a car park.
How many cars are red?

______

2

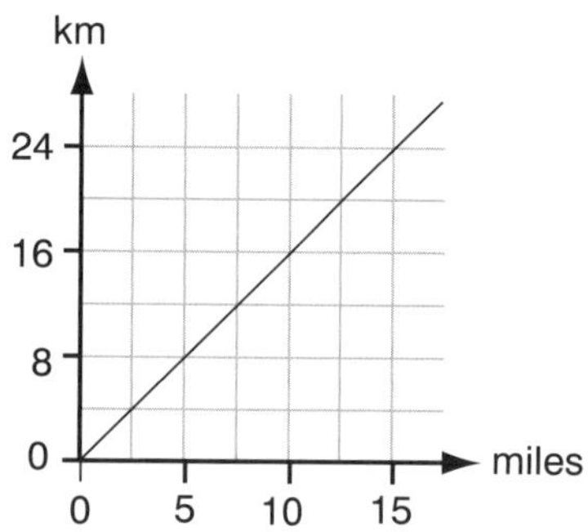

The graph shows the relationship between miles and kilometres.

Complete the following statement:

20 km is equivalent to ______ miles.

3

Alexander collected the following data from 100 pupils.

	Boys	Girls
Reggae	17	29
Hip Hop	13	7
Indipop	12	?

How many girls prefer Indipop music?

______

4

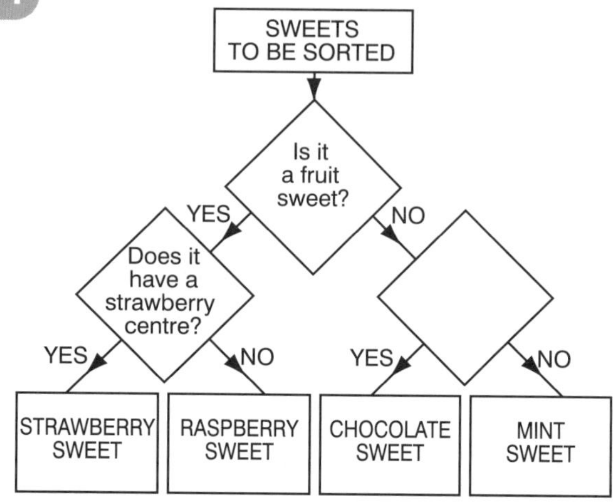

What is missing from the decision tree?
Circle the answer.

A Is it chocolate? **B** Is it mint?

C IT IS MINT. **D** IT IS CHOCOLATE.

E Is it not chocolate?

5

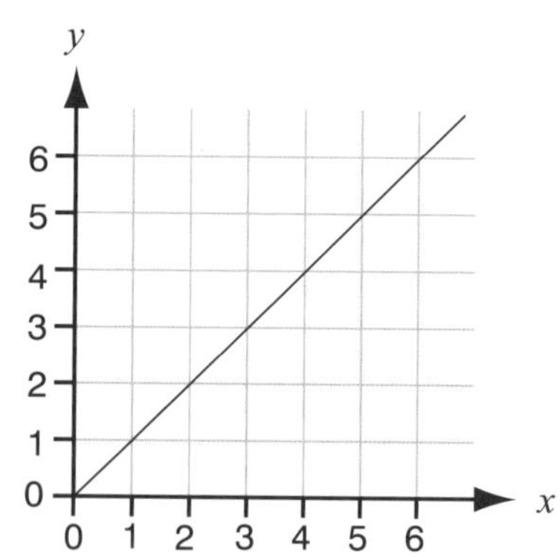

The end points of five lines are given below.
Which line is perpendicular to the line in the diagram?
Circle the answer.

A (1, 2) and (2, 2) **B** (1, 3) and (3, 3)

C (3, 1) and (1, 3) **D** (1, 4) and (4, 2)

E (5, 0) and (1, 3)

6

Bhavesh collected the following data from 100 pupils.

	Boys	Girls
English	19	7
Geography	4	?
Maths	38	30

How many girls preferred geography?

____

7

A bag contains 8 red marbles, 2 green marbles and 10 black marbles.

You pick a marble at random from the bag.

In which of the options below are both statements true?

Circle the answer.

A You have a greater than even chance of picking a black marble.
You have a less than even chance of picking a green marble.

B You have an even chance of picking a black marble.
You have a greater than even chance of picking a red marble.

C You have a greater than even chance of picking a green marble.
You have an even chance of picking a black marble.

D You have a less than even chance of picking a red marble.
You have a less than even chance of picking a green marble.

E You are certain to pick a marble.
You have a greater than even chance of picking a black marble.

8

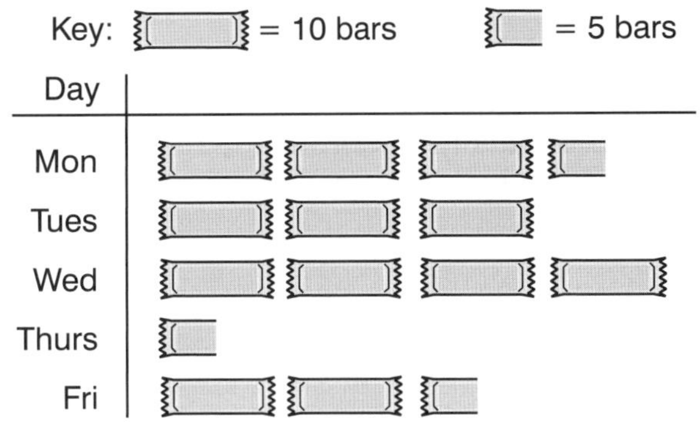

Look at the pictogram above.
How many fruit bars were sold during the whole week?

____

9

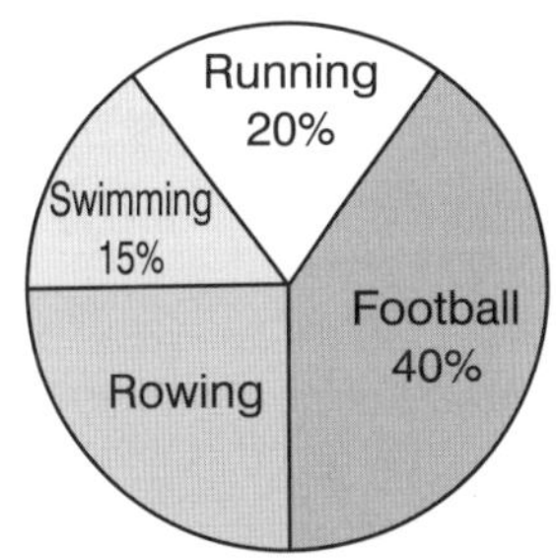

64 children were asked which sports they enjoyed.

How many children liked rowing?

____

10

Look at this table showing the performance of the school cricket team.

Year	Won	Drawn	Lost
2002	7	8	5
2003	13	2	5
2004	6	10	4

How many matches in total did the team not lose?

____

Time for a break! Go to Puzzle Page 43

Total

Test 13: **Number**

Test time: 0 5 10 minutes

1 A coach holds 52 passengers.

12 fully-occupied coaches are required to transport fans to a football match.

How many fans travel by coach?

____

2 A crate can hold 24 cans.

Simon wants to order 312 cans.

How many crates should he order?

____

3

A length of wood is 220 cm long.

It is cut into lengths of 30 cm.

How many complete pieces are made?

____

4

2800 music fans attend a concert.

They travel in coaches. Each coach has 53 seats.

How many coaches are required?

____

5

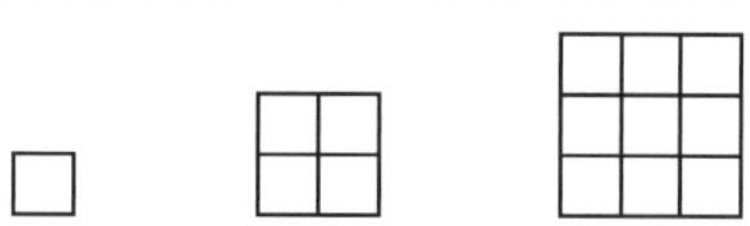

Pattern 1 Pattern 2 Pattern 3

How many tiles will be in Pattern 4?

____

6

Circle the multiple of both 5 and 7.

A 12 **B** 57 **C** 14 **D** 35 **E** 15

7

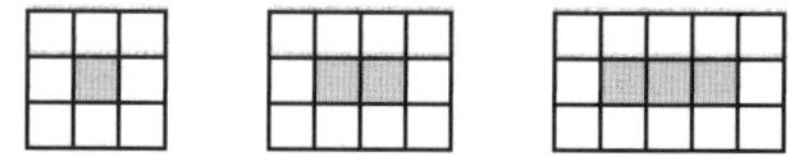

Pattern 1 Pattern 2 Pattern 3

Pattern number	1	2	3	4
Grey tiles	1	2	3	
White tiles	8	10	12	
Total tiles	9	12	15	

Which option correctly completes the details for Pattern 4?

Circle the answer.

A Grey tiles = 4, White tiles = 12, total tiles = 16

B Grey tiles = 3, White tiles = 14, total tiles = 17

C Grey tiles = 4, White tiles = 12, total tiles = 17

D Grey tiles = 4, White tiles = 14, total tiles = 18

E Grey tiles = 4, White tiles = 14, total tiles = 16

8

A drummer beats his drum once every four seconds.

A second drummer beats his drum once every five seconds.

They both start at the same time.

After how many more seconds do they beat their drums together again?

____

9

What is the smallest number divisible by both 8 and 12?

____

10

What is the smallest number that is exactly divisible by 3 and 13?

____

Total

TEST 14: **Algebra**

Test time: 0 5 10 minutes

1

$4a + 2b - 7c = d$.

Find the value of d when $a = 5$, $b = 2$ and $c = 3$.

____

2

$4a + 2b + 3c = 20$

Which of the statements below is incorrect? Circle the answer.

A $8a + 4b + 6c = 40$

B $4a + 2b = 20 - 3c$

C $4a + 2b + 3c - 20 = 0$

D $4a + 2b + 4c = 20 + c$

E $4a = 20 + 2b - 3c$

3

? → [ ] → 168

This machine doubles and then adds 2.

Which number has been put in?

____

4

The length of a rectangle is 8 cm more than its width. Its width is x cm.

A square has a side length of y cm.

The perimeter of the rectangle is larger than that of the square.

How much bigger is the perimeter of the rectangle than that of the square?

Circle the answer.

A $2x + 8 - y$ **B** $4x + 16 - 4y$

C $8x - 4y$ **D** $8xy$ **E** $2x + 8 - 4y$

5

If $17 - 16x = 3 - 2x$, what is the value of x?

____

6

48 → [ ] → ?

This machine divides by 3 and then multiplies by 6.

Which number comes out?

____

7

If $3x + 2 = 2x + 7$, what is the value of x?

____

8

If $32 - x = 23 + 2x$, what is the value of x?

____

9

If Rose had 18 more stamps, she would have four times as many as she actually has.

How many stamps does she have?

____

10

A father's age and his son's age add up to 64. The father is 36 years older than his son.

How old is his son?

____

Total

TEST 15: **Shape and Space**

Test time: 0 5 10 minutes

1–3

Guide the vehicles along the white squares from the start to the finish.

Each vehicle can only move FORWARD, TURN LEFT 90° and TURN RIGHT 90°.

1

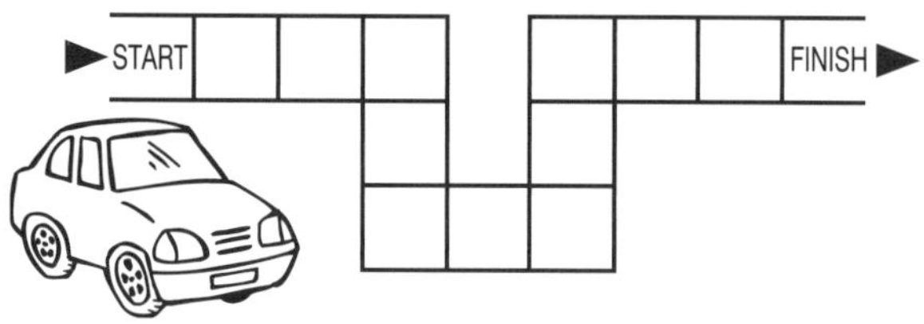

Circle the correct instructions.

A FORWARD 3, TURN LEFT 90°, FORWARD 2, TURN RIGHT 90°, FORWARD 2, TURN LEFT 90°, FORWARD 2, TURN RIGHT 90°, FORWARD 3

B FORWARD 3, TURN RIGHT 90°, FORWARD 2, TURN LEFT 90°, FORWARD 2, TURN LEFT 90°, FORWARD 2, TURN RIGHT 90°, FORWARD 3

C FORWARD 3, TURN RIGHT 90°, FORWARD 2, TURN RIGHT 90°, FORWARD 2, TURN LEFT 90°, FORWARD 2, TURN RIGHT 90°, FORWARD 3

D FORWARD 3, TURN RIGHT 90°, FORWARD 2, TURN RIGHT 90°, FORWARD 2, TURN RIGHT 90°, FORWARD 2, TURN RIGHT 90°, FORWARD 3

E FORWARD 3, TURN LEFT 90°, FORWARD 2, TURN LEFT 90°, FORWARD 2, TURN LEFT 90°, FORWARD 2, TURN LEFT 90°, FORWARD 3

2

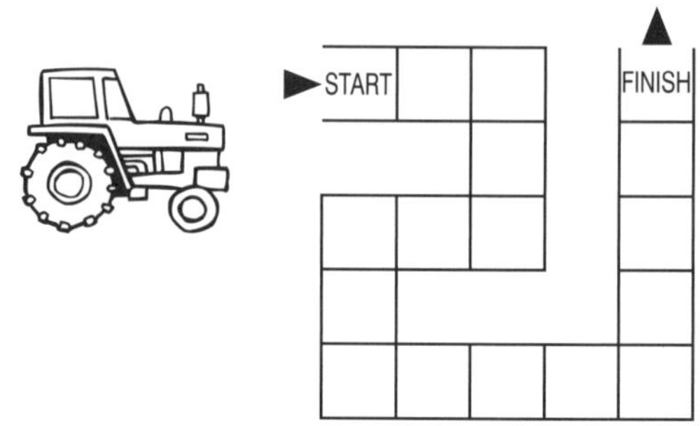

Circle the correct instructions.

A FORWARD 2, TURN RIGHT 90°, FORWARD 2, TURN LEFT 90°, FORWARD 2, TURN RIGHT 90°, FORWARD 2, TURN LEFT 90°, FORWARD 4, TURN LEFT 90°, FORWARD 4

B FORWARD 2, TURN RIGHT 90°, FORWARD 2, TURN RIGHT 90°, FORWARD 2, TURN LEFT 90°, FORWARD 2, TURN RIGHT 90°, FORWARD 4, TURN LEFT 90°, FORWARD 4

C FORWARD 2, TURN RIGHT 90°, FORWARD 2, TURN RIGHT 90°, FORWARD 2, TURN LEFT 90°, FORWARD 2, TURN LEFT 90°, FORWARD 4, TURN LEFT 90°, FORWARD 4

D FORWARD 2, TURN RIGHT 90°, FORWARD 2, TURN LEFT 90°, FORWARD 2, TURN LEFT 90°, FORWARD 2, TURN LEFT 90°, FORWARD 4, TURN LEFT 90°, FORWARD 4

E FORWARD 2, TURN LEFT 90°, FORWARD 2, TURN RIGHT 90°, FORWARD 2, TURN LEFT 90°, FORWARD 2, TURN LEFT 90°, FORWARD 4, TURN LEFT 90°, FORWARD 4

3

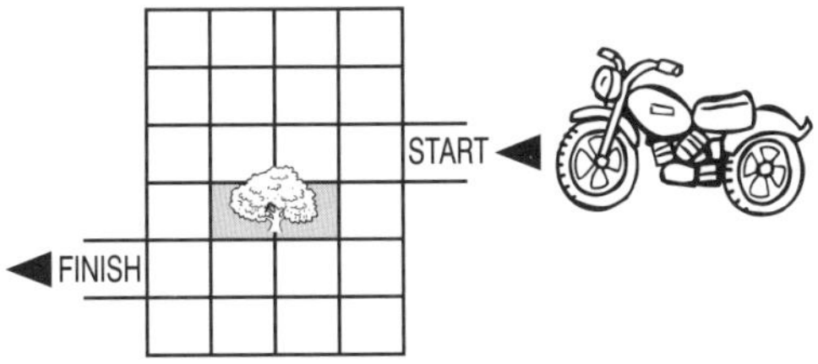

Circle the correct instructions.

A FORWARD 2, TURN LEFT 90°, FORWARD 3, TURN RIGHT 90°, FORWARD 1

B FORWARD 3, TURN LEFT 90°, FORWARD 2, TURN RIGHT 90°, FORWARD 2

C FORWARD 4, TURN LEFT 90°, FORWARD 2, TURN RIGHT 90°, FORWARD 1

D FORWARD 1, TURN LEFT 90°, FORWARD 4, TURN RIGHT 90°, FORWARD 1

E FORWARD 2, TURN LEFT 90°, FORWARD 2, TURN RIGHT 90°, FORWARD 3

4

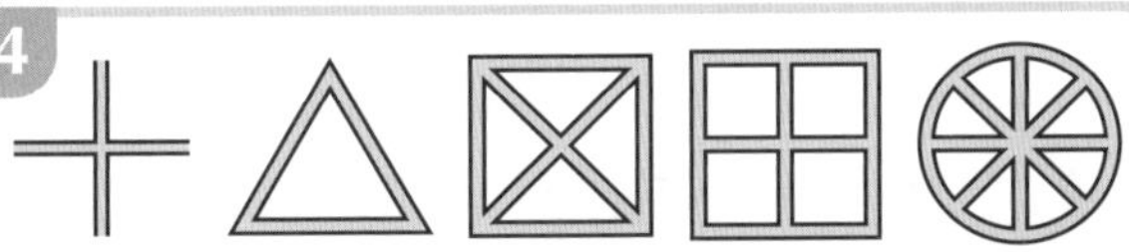

A **B** **C** **D** **E**

A papergirl does not want to visit the same street more than once.

She can pass over the same street corners.

On which housing estate is this possible?

Circle the answer.

5

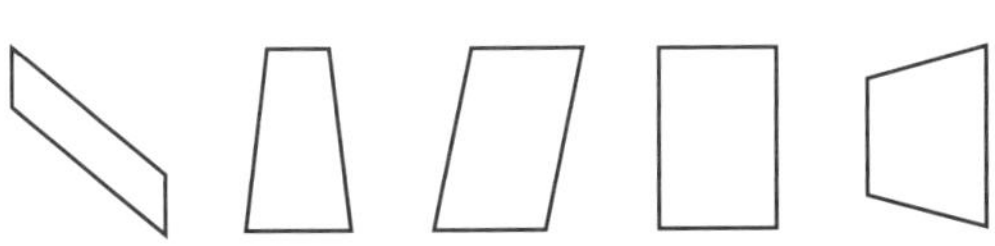

A **B** **C** **D** **E**

Which quadrilateral has four right angles?

Circle the answer.

6

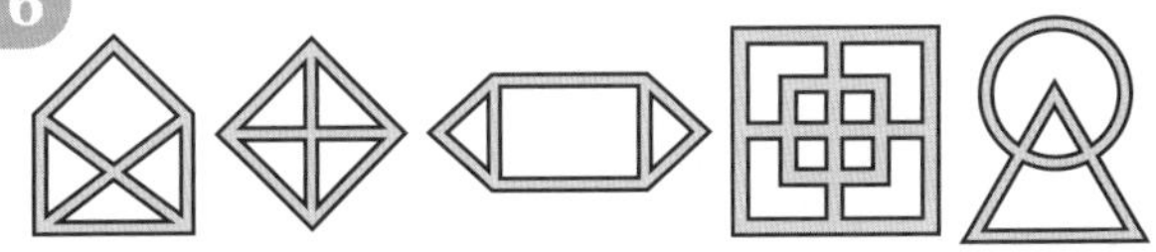

A **B** **C** **D** **E**

A postman does not want to visit the same street more than once.

He can pass over the same street corners.

On which housing estate is this possible?

Circle the answer.

7

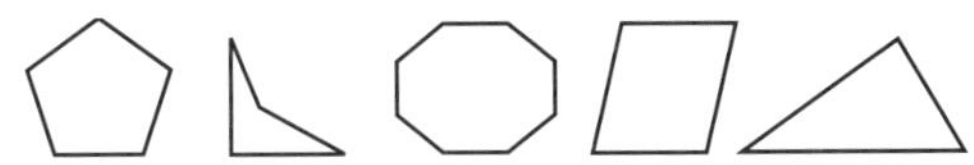

A **B** **C** **D** **E**

Which polygon has an internal reflex angle?

Circle the answer.

8

The diagram shows a rectangle joined to an equilateral triangle.

Find the size of the angle marked x.

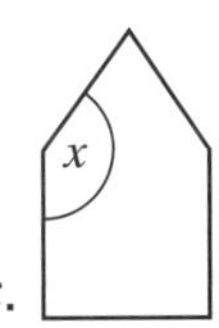

__________ °

9

One of the angles of this scalene triangle is 30°.

The other angle is 80°.

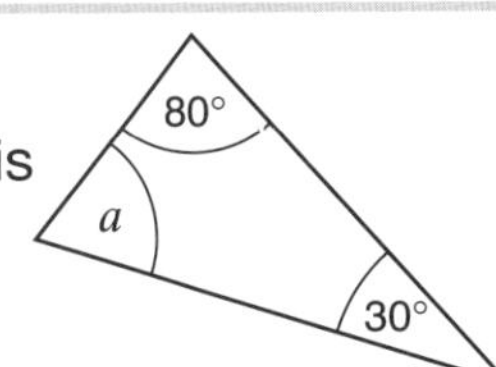

Find the size of the third angle marked a.

__________ °

10

What is the approximate size of the angle marked b in this rhombus?

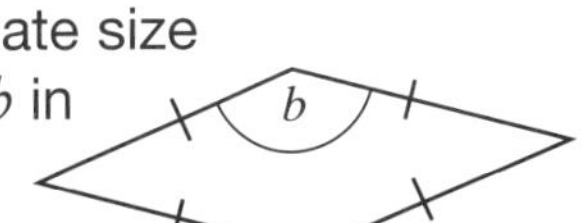

Circle the answer.

A 260° **B** 40° **C** 180° **D** 140° **E** 310°

Total

TEST 16: **Mixed**

Test time: 0 5 10 minutes

1

Given that $4x + 2y$ is the total cost in pounds for four adults and two children to enter a museum, which of the following statements is correct?

Circle the correct answer.

The cost for four adults and two children to enter the museum can also be written as:

A $8xy$ **B** $42xy$ **C** $6xy$

D $2(2x + y)$ **E** $8xy^2$

2

Which letter shows two prime numbers that add up to make a square number?

Circle the answer.

A 12 and 13 **B** 17 and 19 **C** 16 and 20

D 16 and 8 **E** 1 and 35

3

435 pupils are put into classes of 23 pupils. How many complete classes are there?

____

4

If $6x + 7 = 28 - x$, what is the value of x?

____

5

How many minutes are there in total in 4 hours and 32 minutes?

____

6

Kevin wants to estimate the length of a room.

It takes him 15 strides to walk the length of the room.

What is the approximate length of the room?

Circle the answer.

A 40 m **B** 1400 mm **C** 1400 cm

D 200 cm **E** 3 km

7

The cost of a ham roll is £x and the cost of a tuna salad is £y.

Brian orders 5 ham rolls and 3 tuna salads.

What is a correct expression for the total cost of his order?

Circle the answer.

A $53xy$ **B** $5x + 3y$ **C** $15xy$

D $8xy$ **E** $15(x + y)$

8 Write in words the number 14 205.

____

____

9 4.3201

What is this number to two decimal places?

____

10 14 9 22 7 21

These are the number of letters received by a library each day for a week.

What is the median number of letters?

____

Total

Test 17: **Mixed**

Test time: 0 5 10 minutes

1

Here is part of a conversion table.
Which figure is missing from the table?

lbs	g	kg	lbs
5	2268	5	11.02
6	2722	6	?
7	3175	7	15.43
8	3629	8	17.64

____

2 13 14 15 16 18

Circle the number which is divisible by both 3 and 5.

3

What proportion of 3 hours is 10 minutes?

Circle the answer.

A $\frac{1}{3}$ **B** $\frac{1}{6}$ **C** $\frac{1}{18}$ **D** $\frac{1}{9}$ **E** $\frac{1}{12}$

4 DUD FUF EEE POP DOL

Which of these has a horizontal line of symmetry? Circle the answer.

5–6

Where is the court?

(____ , ____)

Where is the fire station?

(____ , ____)

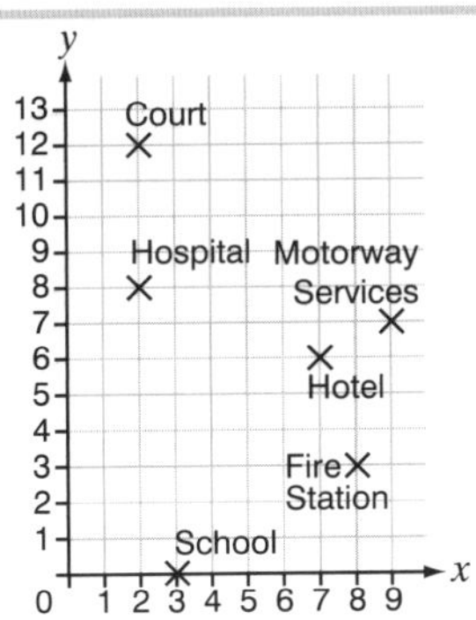

7

64 → ÷8 → ×5 → __________

Complete the function machine.

8

Edward has these coins in his pocket.

1p 2p 5p 10p 10p 10p 10p £1

He selects a coin at random.

In which of the options below are both statements true?

Circle the answer.

A He has an even chance of picking a 10p coin out.
He has an even chance of picking a coin less than 10p out.

B He has a less than even chance of picking a 2p coin out.
He has a less than even chance of picking a 5p coin out.

C He has an even chance of picking a 1p coin out.
He is certain to pick a coin of value £1 or less.

D He has an even chance of picking a 10p coin out.
He has an even chance of picking a coin out greater than 10p.

E He is certain to pick a coin out that is less than £1.
He has a less than even chance of picking a coin out that is less than 10p.

9 Which of these will hold about 10 litres?

Circle the answer.

A a teaspoon **B** a cup

C a swimming pool **D** a bucket

E a lake

10 What fraction is 10 mm of 30 cm?

Circle the answer.

A $\frac{1}{3}$ **B** $\frac{1}{30}$ **C** $\frac{10}{30}$ **D** $\frac{1}{300}$ **E** $\frac{1}{0.3}$

Total

Test time: 0 5 10 minutes

Test 18: **Mixed**

1

A length of wire is d cm long.

It is cut to form an equilateral triangle of side x cm **and** a square of side y cm.

The perimeter of the equilateral triangle and the square are the same.

Read these statements.

Statement 1: $6x = d$

Statement 2: $8y = d$

Statement 3: $4x + 3y = d$

Circle the answer.

A All of the statements are correct.

B Only statement 3 is correct.

C Only statements 1 and 2 are correct.

2

Sam buys some apples which cost 27p each.

He pays for them with three one pound coins.

Kay buys the same number of bananas which cost 37p each.

She pays for them with four one pound coins.

They each receive the same amount of change.

How many pieces of fruit did each person buy?

____

3

A canteen makes 456 pies.

They sell 322.

How many pies remain?

____

4

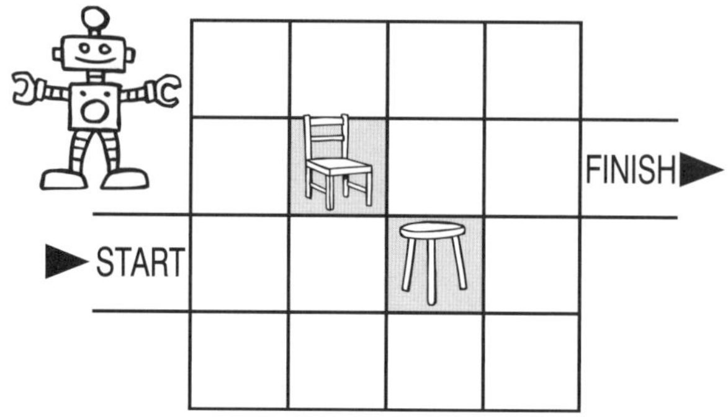

Guide the robot through the kitchen without hitting any hazards.

He can only move FORWARD, TURN LEFT 90° and TURN RIGHT 90°.

Circle the correct instructions.

A FORWARD 1, TURN RIGHT 90°, FORWARD 1, TURN RIGHT 90°, FORWARD 1

B FORWARD 2, TURN LEFT 90°, FORWARD 1, TURN RIGHT 90°, FORWARD 3

C FORWARD 2, TURN RIGHT 90°, FORWARD 1, TURN LEFT 90°, FORWARD 2, TURN LEFT 90°, FORWARD 2, TURN RIGHT 90°, FORWARD 1

D FORWARD 3, TURN RIGHT 90°, FORWARD 1, TURN LEFT 90°, FORWARD 2, TURN LEFT 90°, FORWARD 1, TURN RIGHT 90°, FORWARD 1

E FORWARD 3, TURN LEFT 90°, FORWARD 1, TURN LEFT 90°, FORWARD 2, TURN LEFT 90°, FORWARD 2, TURN RIGHT 90°, FORWARD 1

Test 1: Shape and Space (pp2–3)

1 $\frac{1}{8}$ 60 minutes = 1 hour, so 2 × 60 = 120 minutes. 15 minutes out of 120 minutes is $\frac{15}{120}$. Simplify the fraction by dividing the numerator (top number) and denominator (bottom number) by the same number. The digits in the fraction are large, so do this in a couple of steps: 15 and 120 can both be divided by 5 and simplified to $\frac{3}{24}$; simplify again by dividing by 3 to get $\frac{1}{8}$.

2 **C** To change 24-hour clock into 12-hour clock, subtract 12 from the hours if they are between 13:00 and 23:59: 21 – 12 = 9, so it is 9.42. 00:00 to 11:59 is a.m. and 12:00 to 23:59 is p.m., so 21:42 is 9.42 p.m.

3 **B** First, add the missing numbers along the bottom (*x*-axis) and up the side (*y*-axis). Both have 10 increments between 0 and 1, so take the difference between these numbers (= 1) and divide it by the number of increments (1 ÷ 10 = 0.1). Then label each increment (e.g. 0.1, 0.2, 0.3, etc.). Write the increments on the grid, increasing by 0.1 each time: decimal numbers increase in the same way as whole numbers, so 0.1 is followed by 0.2, 0.3, 0.4 and so on.
To write co-ordinates, use the phrase 'along the corridor and up the stairs'. This means along the *x*-axis then up the *y*-axis, so this number is second.

4–8 Refer to Question 3.

4 **(8.2, 8.5)** There are 10 increments between 8 and 9, so they will increase by 0.1 each time. The first number is 8 and will be followed by 8.1, 8.2, 8.3 and so on.

5 **(6, 7)**

6 **(5, 8)**

7 **A**

8 **C**

9–10 Whereas only one quadrant was shown in Question 3–8, four quadrants are shown here and –4 to 4 is also shown on each axis. Continue to use 'along the corridor and up the stairs' to write the co-ordinates in the correct order.

9 **E**

10 **(2, –2)** The sides of the square shown are 4 ones along and upwards: draw a line 4 squares downwards from B and a line 4 squares across from D to find (2, –2).

Test 2: Number (p4)

1 **A** Write the number in a place value grid to help write it in words.

10 000s	1000s	100s	10s	Ones
5	9	0	3	8

2–3 Use the place value grid shown in Question 1.

2 **90 909** Make sure zeros are included as 'place-holders'. For example, the number 909 needs a 0 otherwise it becomes 99, a completely different number.

3 **E** The 3 will be in the thousands column, so it is worth three thousand.

4 **A** Decimal numbers increase in the same way as whole numbers, for example, 2.3 is followed by 2.4, 2.5, 2.6 and so on; 2.38 is followed by 2.39, 2.40, 2.41 and so on. Only 2.40 is between 2.39 and 2.42.

5 **300** or **3 hundreds** The number has been multiplied by 10 each time. When a number is multiplied by 10, 100, 1000, etc, it is moved to the left on a place value grid: as 10 has one zero, it is moved 1 place each time (if multiplying by 100, it would be moved 2 places, as 100 has two zeros, and so on). Add a zero in the ones, tens, hundreds, etc, if they are left empty. 130 × 10 = 1 300 and 1 300 × 10 = 13 000. The 3 in the missing number is in the hundreds column.

100000s	10000s	1000s	100s	10s	ones
			1	3	0
		1	3	0	0
	1	3	0	0	0

6 **7.006** Place the numbers in a grid, ensuring the decimal points are aligned. Add a zero in any gaps after the decimal point, so all the numbers have the same amount of digits after it (7.6 is the same as 7.600, 7.06 is the same as 7.060, etc.). Look for the smallest number in the first column: if they are all the same, go onto the next column and so on.

7	•	6	0	0
7	•	0	6	0
7	•	6	0	0
7	•	0	0	6
7	•	6	0	0

7 $\frac{2}{3}$ 11 girls out of 30 pupils is $\frac{11}{30}$. When making approximations, numbers are rounded. In the fraction $\frac{11}{30}$, 30 is already rounded to the nearest 10 but 11 needs to be rounded. To do this, identify the digit in the place value column you are rounding to and look at the digit that follows it: if it is 4 or less, just change it to zero; if it is 5 or more, change it to zero and increase the number in the column you are rounding to by 1. The 1 in the ones in 11 is rounded to 0 and the 1 in the tens column remains the same: 11

becomes 10 and the fraction is changed to $\frac{10}{30}$. This is the number of girls.

The whole class is $\frac{30}{30}$, so subtract $\frac{10}{30}$ from this to find the number of boys: $\frac{30}{30} - \frac{10}{30} = \frac{20}{30}$. When subtracting fractions, only subtract the numerators (top numbers) and leave the denominator (bottom numbers) the same. $\frac{20}{30}$ can be simplified to $\frac{2}{3}$ (refer to Test 1 Q 1 on simplifying fractions).

8 **$\frac{4}{5}$** Write the proportions as fractions: the whole amount is $\frac{2500}{2500}$ and the concentrate is $\frac{500}{2500}$. First, simplify the fractions (refer to Test 1 Q 1) by dividing by 100. When a number is divided by 10, 100, 1000, etc, it is moved to the right on a place value grid: as 100 has two zeros, move it 2 places (if it were 1000, it would move 3 places and so on). 2500 ÷ 100 = 25 and 500 ÷ 100 = 5, so the fractions become $\frac{25}{25}$ and $\frac{5}{25}$. Simplify further to get $\frac{5}{5}$ and $\frac{1}{5}$ then subtract: $\frac{5}{5} - \frac{1}{5} = \frac{4}{5}$ (refer to Q 7 on subtracting fractions).

1000s	100s	10s	ones	Decimal Point	10s	100s
2	5	0	0	•		
		2	5	•	0	0
	5	0	0	•		
			5	•	0	0

9–10 Refer to Question 7 on rounding.

9 **7.63** A number with 2 decimal places has two digits after the decimal point: 3 is followed by 2. As that is less than 4, the 3 remains the same and is rounded to 7.63.

10 **9.00** 9 is two places after the decimal and followed by 5, so the 9 needs to increase by 1. When the digit 9 is increased, it becomes 0 and the digit to its left is increased by 1. However, this digit is also 9, so the same thing happens again: 9 becomes a 0 and the digit to its left is increased by 1, so 8 becomes 9. As the number is being rounded to two decimal places, it still needs two digits after the decimal, even if they are zeros.

Test 3: Shape and Space (p 5)

1 **D** Look at the corner of each shape: the smallest gap shown on the interior of a corner is in the triangle.

2 **E** Diagonals are straight lines that go from corner to corner on a 2D shape.

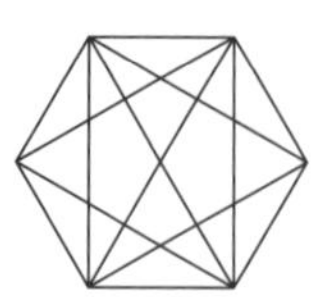

3 **SIH** A full turn is 360°, so a half-turn is 180°. Turn the page upside down (a half-turn) to find the answer.

4 **D** If a shape looks exactly the same after it has been rotated, then it has rotational symmetry. Only option D is able to do this.

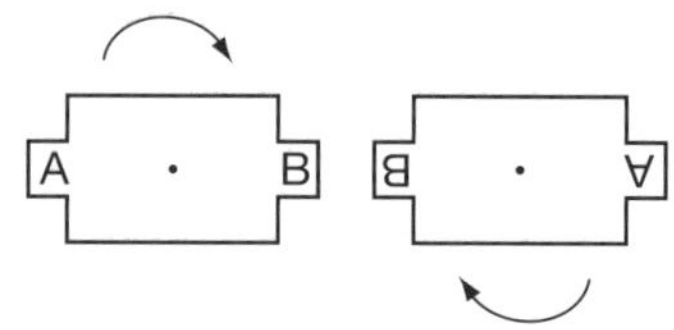

5 **LAL** Vertical lines of symmetry will be through the centre, running from top to bottom. A mirror image of the letters needs to be shown to the left and right of the line of symmetry.

MUM TAT HAH LAL XOX

6 **DID** Horizontal lines of symmetry will be through the centre, running from left to right. A mirror image of the letters needs to be shown above and below the line of symmetry.

DID CAT HUH NUN TAT

7–8 **44, 32** First, find the missing lengths by separating the shape into rectangles:

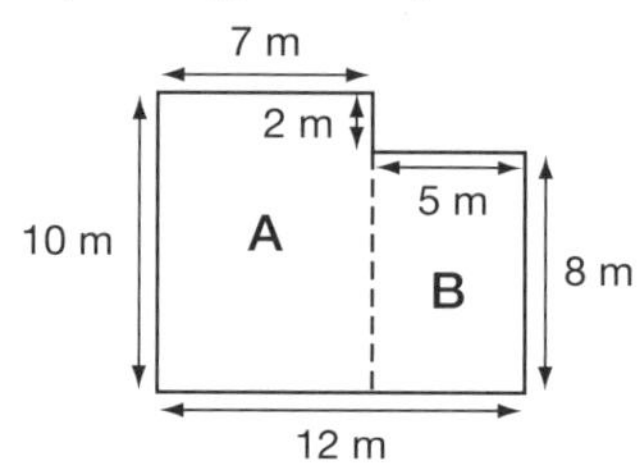

Use the measurements given on the opposite sides to calculate the missing ones. The perimeter of a shape is the total length around the outside: 10 + 7 + 2 + 5 + 8 + 12 = 44.

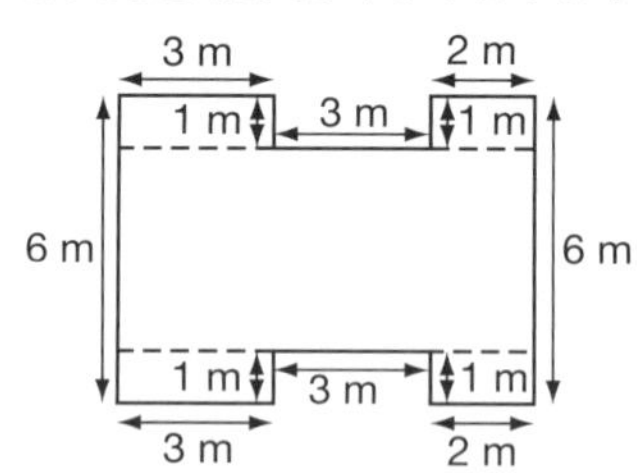

Find the missing dimensions using subtraction. The perimeter is 6 + 3 + 1 + 3 + 1 + 2 + 6 + 2 + 1 + 3 + 1 + 3 = 32.

9 **D** Shapes A, B and E are all regular shapes, so each of their sides are the same length. A is 3 × 4 = 12; B is 4 × 3 = 12; E is 6 × 2 = 12. In shapes C and D, the opposite sides are the same length: C = 2 + 2 + 4 + 4 = 12; D = 1 + 1 + 6 + 6 = 14.

10 **A** All the sides are the same length and the missing length is represented with *a*. There are 12 sides and $12 \times a$ is written as $12a$ in algebra because the '×' sign is not used.

Test 4: Data Handling (pp6–7)

1 **40** One full bar represents 10 and 4 full bars shown for Wednesday. $4 \times 10 = 40$

2 **A** 39 were sold on Monday $(6 \times 6) + 3 = 39$) and 27 were sold on Wednesday $(4 \times 6) + 3 = 27$); $39 - 27 = 12$.

3–4 Align a ruler with the top of the bars to see which numbers they are level with on the *y*-axis.

3 **5** 7 were bought on Tuesday and 12 on Friday. $12 - 7 = 5$

4 **28** The bar for Maths is level with 30. The bar for Geography is just below half-way between 0 and 5 (2.5 or $2\frac{1}{2}$), so it represents 2 pupils: $30 - 2 = 28$.

5 **7** 6 pupils completed 21–30 laps and 1 pupil completed 31–40 laps: $6 + 1 = 7$.

6 **23** 20 pupils scored 20–29; 1 pupil scored 30–39; and 2 pupils scored 40–49: $20 + 1 + 2 = 23$.

6–10 Probability is the chance of something happening out of a total number of possible outcomes. For example, on a dice, the number 5 has 1 chance out of 6 of being thrown as there is only 1 number 5 on a dice and a dice has 6 sides. This can be written as 1 in 6 or $\frac{1}{6}$. When comparing possible outcomes, it is best to write them as fractions on a number line. (Remember that $\frac{1}{2}$ is the same as an even chance and all possible outcomes always add up to 1).

7 **C** Find the total amount of marbles to find how many possible outcomes there are: $2 + 4 + 6 = 12$ possible outcomes. As there are 12, mark the possibilities on a number line as twelfths: red is 2 out of 12 $(\frac{2}{12})$, green is 4 out 12 $(\frac{4}{12})$ and yellow is 6 out of 12 $(\frac{6}{12})$. As $\frac{6}{12}$ can be simplified to $\frac{1}{2}$, it is the same as an even chance.

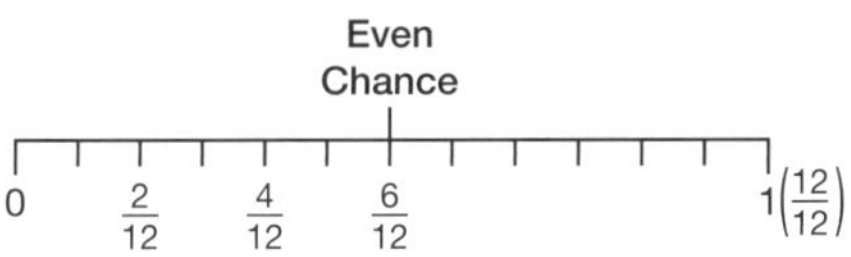

8 **B** There are 6 sides on a dice, so mark the possibilities on a number line as sixths: rolling an even number is $\frac{3}{6}$ as there are 3 even numbers; rolling a number less than six is $\frac{5}{6}$ as there are 5 numbers less than 6; rolling a prime number is $\frac{3}{6}$ as there are 3 prime numbers (2, 3 and 5) and so on. A prime number is a number that can only be divided by the number 1 and itself. For example, 7 is a prime number as it can only be divided by 1 and 7 (1 is not a prime number as it cannot be divided by 1 and another number).

9 $\mathbf{\frac{21}{23}}$ $3 + 2 + 5 + 6 + 7 = 23$ balls. Subtract the number of red balls to find the possibility of not picking one: $23 - 2 = 21$, so the chance is $\frac{21}{23}$.

10 **0.75** or $\mathbf{\frac{3}{4}}$ or **75%** There are 4 different numbers, so 4 possible outcomes. 3 of those numbers are greater than 1, so the chance is 3 out of 4 $(\frac{3}{4})$. Equivalent answers of 0.75 and 75% are also acceptable.

Test 5: Number (p8)

1–4 A square number is a number that is multiplied by itself. For example, 4^2 is $4 \times 4 = 16$, so 16 is a square number. A cubed number is a number that is multiplied by itself, then multiplied by itself again. For example, 2^3 is the same as $2 \times 2 \times 2 = 8$ so 8 is a cubed number. Write a list of square and cubed numbers up to 16 to help answer the questions. Refer to Test 4 Q 8 on prime numbers.

1 **15** 2 **1**

3 **A** Only option A shows two prime numbers: $3 + 5 = 8$, which is 2^3.

4 **4** Odd numbers are shown in an increasing order, so Line 6 would show: $1 + 3 + 5 + 7 + 9 + 11 = 36$: 3, 5, 7 and 11 are prime numbers.

5–10 Use column addition and column subtraction. When using column addition, work from right to left and make sure any numbers carried over are added on in the next column. When using column subtraction, make sure the larger number is at the top. Work from right to left and make sure you exchange from the next column if the number above is bigger than the one below if the number above it is smaller.
If calculating decimals, line them up so that they are in the same column and place a decimal in the answer space, aligned with the others, to make sure it is in the correct place in the answer. Add a 0 to any places that are left empty.

5 **283** Subtract the total number of people who preferred curries and stir-fries from 567: $78 + 206 = 284$ and $567 - 284 = 283$.

$$\begin{array}{rccc} & 2 & 0 & 6 \\ + & & 7 & 8 \\ \hline & 2 & 8 & 4 \\ \hline & & 1 & \end{array}$$

$$\begin{array}{rccc} & {}^{4}\not{5} & {}^{1}6 & 7 \\ - & 2 & 8 & 4 \\ \hline & 2 & 8 & 3 \\ \hline \end{array}$$

6 **6** Subtract the total amount of children acting and assisting backstage from 127: $72 + 49 = 121$; $127 - 121 = 6$.

7–8 **258, 42** 986 – 728 = 258. Find the new total of meals and subtract 986: 728 + 300 = 1028; 1028 – 986 = 42.

	0~~1~~	9~~0~~	12	8
–		9	8	6
		0	4	2

9 **21** Find the total of people that get on and the total that get off, then subtract to find how many are left: 35 + 14 + 12 + 6 = 67 get on, 2 + 16 + 28 = 46 get off; 67 – 46 = 21.

10 **£53.63** Subtract £5.00 from £58.63.

	5	8	•	6	3
–		5	•	0	0
	5	3	•	6	3

Test 6: Data Handling (p 9)

The mode is the number that occurs the most often. To find the median, write the numbers in order from smallest to largest: the number in the middle is the median. To find the mean, add all the numbers together, then divide by the amount of numbers you have added. The range is the difference between the smallest and largest number.

1 **27** 27 occurs most often.

2 **Purple** Most pupils chose purple, so this is the modal colour.

3 **D** £110, £120, £130, £140, £150, £220, £435: £140 is in the middle.

4 **40 000** Divide 960 000 by 24 to find the mean. Use short division to complete the sum. 24 does not go into 9, so write a zero above it and carry the 9 over to the next column to create the number 96. 24 goes into 96 four times, so write 4 above 96 (use repeated addition: 24 + 24 + 24 + 24 = 96 (4 lots of 24). 24 goes into zero 0 times, so write 0 above the remaining digits.

	0	4	0	0	0	0
2 4	9	9 6	0	0	0	0

5 **E** 199 – 174 = 25 (refer to Test 5 Q 5–10 on column subtraction).

6 **A** 8 – 0 = 8

7 **C** 13 – 1 = 12

8 **B** 5, 7, 12, 19, 20: 12 is in the middle.

9 **12** The total number of cups has been divided by 5 days to get the answer of 7 (35 ÷ 5 = 7). The number of cups needs to add up to 35. Add the numbers shown for each day and subtract from 35 to find the answer: 35 – (2 + 8 + 9 + 4) = 35 – 23 = 12.

10 **8** Refer to Question 9. Find the mean: 45 ÷ 5 = 9; find the missing number: 45 – (12 + 13 + 8 + 4) = 45 – 37 = 8.

Test 7: Shape and Space (pp 10–11)

1 **D** Copy and cut out the nets shown, then assemble each to find the answer.

2 **D** Use column multiplication to find 30 × 30 = 900. Then, multiply 900 by the number of squares in the shape using long multiplication: 25 × 900 = 22 500.

			9	0	0
×				2	5
		4	5	0	0
+	1	8	0	0	0
	2	2	5	0	0
	1				

The answer is in m^2: 100 cm = 1 metre, so 1 m^2 = 100 cm × 100 cm = 10 000 cm, so divide 22 500 by 10 000 to change it into m^2. 22 500 ÷ 10 000 = 2.25 (refer to Test 2 Q 5 on dividing by powers of 10).

3 **35** To find the area of a parallelogram, use length × height: 7 × 5 = 35.

4 **A** Separate the shape into a rectangle and two triangles: the area of a rectangle is width × length; the area of a triangle base × height ÷ 2. In this question the *y* is a 'red herring' and not needed to calculate the answer.

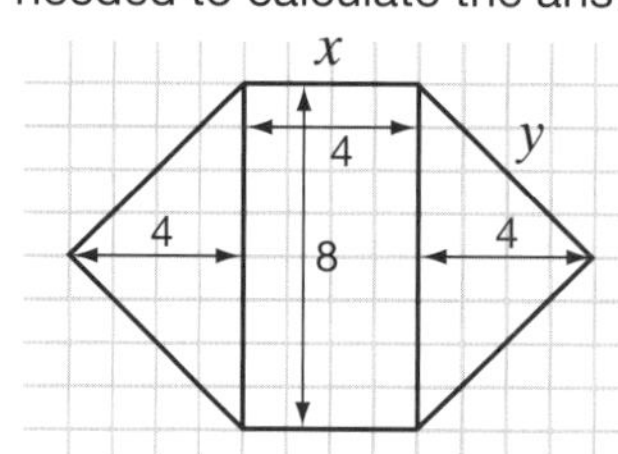

x = 4 squares. The length of the rectangle is 8, which is 2 lots of 4 (2 lots of x), and can be written as $2x$. Therefore, the area of the rectangle x times $2x$, which is $2x^2$ (x times x = x^2).

The height of each triangle is 4 = x (imagine the triangles turned on their side). The base of each triangle is 8, which is $2x$. Therefore, the area is x times $2x$ divided by 2: x times $2x = 2x^2$ and $2x^2$ ÷ 2 = $1x^2$, which is written as x^2 (1 is not used with a letter in algebra).

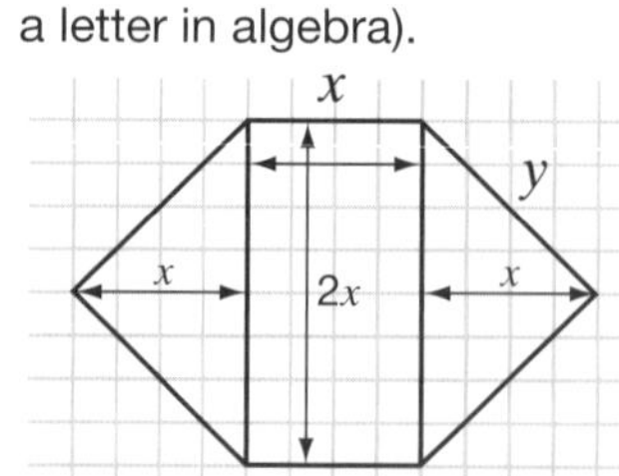

The total area of the shape is found by adding the measurements together, so: $2x^2$ (rectangle) + x^2 (first triangle) + x^2 (second triangle) = $4x^2$.

5 **4** Draw the smaller triangle inside the larger one, carefully measuring half-way along the side of the larger triangle.

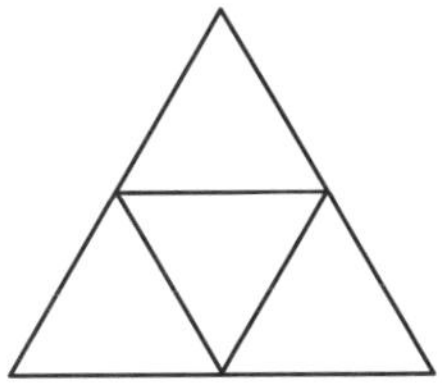

6 **D** Copy and cut out the nets shown, then assemble each to find the answer.

7–10 Refer to Question 4 on finding the area of a rectangle and triangle. The perimeter of a shape is the total length around the outside.

7 **24** $4 \times 12 \div 2 = 24$. Group the items to make the sum easier: 4×6 may be easier to calculate than $48 \div 2$.

8 **7.5** The base of the triangle is the same as the length of the rectangle and the height is the same as its width, so 15 just needs to be divided by 2 (refer to Test 6 Q 4 on short division).

9 **E** Find all the factors pairs of 70 to see which numbers could have been multiplied together to get an area of 70 cm^2. Factor pairs are two numbers that are multiplied together to make another number. 1 and 70, 2 and 35, 5 and 14, 7 and 10 are all factor pairs of 70. To find which pair has been used to calculate the area, add the numbers in each pair together and multiply by 2 (remember that a rectangle has 2 pairs of sides of equal length). Only $7 + 7 + 10 + 10$ gives one of the answers shown (34).

10 **C** Two sides are 10 cm, subtract this from 24 to give 4. If both widths = 4 cm, then one width = 2 cm and 10 cm × 2 cm = 20 cm^2.

Test 8: Number (p12)

1–4 To compare fractions, decimals and percentages, convert all the options shown into decimals and write them in a decimal grid (as shown below in Question 1). To convert fractions into decimals, divide the numerator (top number) by the denominator (bottom number) using short division (refer to Test 6 Q 4). For example, $\frac{1}{2}$ is $1 \div 2 = 0.5$. To convert percentages into decimals, write the numbers in the percentage after the decimal point, e.g. 25% = 0.25.

1 **$\frac{4}{9}$** $\frac{1}{2} = 0.5$, $\frac{6}{10} = 0.6$, $\frac{3}{5} = 0.6$, $\frac{4}{9} = 0.444$ and $\frac{5}{8} = 0.625$. Align the decimals in a grid. Look for the smallest number in the first column: if they are all the same go onto the next column, and so on. 0.444 is the smallest here, the equivalent of $\frac{4}{9}$.

0	•	5	0	0
0	•	6	0	0
0	•	6	0	0
0	•	4	4	4
0	•	6	2	5

2 **$\frac{2}{5}$** $\frac{2}{5} = 0.4$, 20% = 0.20, $\frac{1}{3} = 0.33$, 35% = 0.35. Place in a grid, as shown in Question 1: 0.4 is the largest, the equivalent of $\frac{2}{5}$.

3–4 To find a fraction of the number, divide the number by the denominator (bottom number) in the fraction and multiply the answer by the numerator (top number). For example, $\frac{3}{4}$ of 200 is: $200 \div 4 = 50$ then $50 \times 3 = 150$, so $\frac{3}{4}$ of 200 = 150.

3 **D** Knowledge of common fraction, percentages and decimal equivalents is needed here. $\frac{3}{4}$, 75% and 0.75 are the same value, so options A, B and C will produce the same answer: all are 150. To calculate option D, '0.5 of' is equivalent to '$\frac{1}{2}$ times': $\frac{1}{2} \times 400 = 200$. To find 150% in option E, partition 150 into 100 and 50: 100% is the full amount (100 here); 50% is the equivalent of $\frac{1}{2}$, which is 50; 100 + 50 = 150.

4 **D** Use knowledge of common fraction, percentages and decimal equivalents here. 62% is 0.62 so A is less than B. $\frac{3}{5} = 0.6$ or 60%, also less than B. $\frac{2}{3}$ is 0.67 or 67% (rounded) – now D is larger than B. For option E, $\frac{1}{8}$ is 0.125, $\frac{5}{8}$ is $5 \times 0.125 = 0.625$ or 62.5% so this is less than D.

5–7 To change a fraction into a percentage, find the equivalent fraction with a denominator of 100 by multiplying the numerator (top number) and denominator (bottom number) by the same number. The numerator is the percentage. For example, $\frac{1}{5}$ can be changed to $\frac{20}{100}$ by multiplying both numbers by 20 and $\frac{20}{100}$ = 20%.

5 **68%** 17 out of 25 is $\frac{17}{25}$: to find the percentage, $\frac{17}{25} \times 100$, simplify by dividing the 100 and 25 to give 17×4 = 68%.

6 **40%** 6 out of 15 boxes are shaded = $\frac{6}{15}$ which can be simplified to $\frac{2}{5}$ (refer to Test 1 Q 1 on simplifying fractions). To find the percentage, $\frac{2}{5} \times 100 = 2 \times 20$ = 40%.

7 **74%** $50 - 13 = 37$, so he has $\frac{37}{50}$ left: to find the percentage, simplify $\frac{37}{50} \times 100$ to give 37×2 = 74%.

8 **80** Refer to Question 4 on finding the percentage of a number: $400 \times \frac{20}{100}$ and simplify to $4 \times 20 = 80$.

9 **£1200** $\frac{1}{3}$ of £1800 = £600; £1800 – £600 = £1200.

10 **280** The fraction is shown in tenths, so the whole 1400 is $\frac{10}{10}$ and $\frac{10}{10} - \frac{8}{10} = \frac{2}{10}$. Therefore, $\frac{2}{10}$ bought other brands (refer to Test 2 Q 7 on subtracting fractions). $\frac{2}{10}$ of 1400 = $\frac{2}{10} \times 1400$ = 2 × 140 = 280.

Test 9: Shape and Space (p 13)

1–2 To find the volume, multiply the length by the width by the height.

1 **250** 10 × 5 = 50 and 50 × 5 = 250

2 **0.5** 2 × 0.5 = 1 and 1 × 0.5 = 0.5

3 **6.26** Refer to Test 2 Q 4 on decimal numbers.

4–5 Refer to Test 5 Q 5–10 on column addition and subtraction.

4 **D** 1 kg is approximately the same weight as 1 litre: 2 litres × 3 = 6 litres; 6 litres + 1.5 litres + 1 kg = 8.5 kg (6.0 + 1.5 + 1.0 = 8.5).

5 **A** 1000 g = 1 kg, so convert 850 g into kg by dividing by 1000: 850 ÷ 1000 = 0.850 kg (refer to Test 2 Q 8 on dividing by powers of 10). 25.800 – 0.850 = 24.950 = 24.95

6 **E** Use knowledge of the height or length of items you are familiar with, e.g. the height of a door is approximately 2 metres, so a tall man is approximately 2 metres tall. 6 × 2 m = 12 m.

7 **C** Use knowledge of the weight of items you are familiar with, e.g. a large bottle of water is 1.5 litres, so 50 litres is the most appropriate measurement.

8 **B** Refer to Question 7.

9 **70** Separate the shape into two rectangles and add the missing measurements (refer to Test 3 Q 7–8). Find the area of each rectangle, by multiplying the length by the width, and add the answers together to find the total area. There are two options here: (8 × 5) + (6 × 5) = 70 or (2 × 5) + (6 × 10) = 70. One of these is easier than the other to calculate quickly.

10 **D** The large triangle is made up of 9 triangles the same size as the shaded one: 9 × 1000 = 9000 mm². However, this is not one of the options given in mm2, so convert this into cm². 10 mm = 1 cm, so 1cm² = 10 mm × 10 mm = 100 mm, so divide by 100 to convert it into cm²: 9000 ÷ 100 = 90.

Test 10: Number (p 14)

1–5 Refer to Test 8 Q 3–4 on finding a fraction of a number and Test 2 Q 7 on subtracting fractions.

1 **16** (24 ÷ 3) × 2 = 16

2 **120** (300 ÷ 5) × 2 = 120

3 **175** The whole amount of 250 can be written as $\frac{10}{10}$ and $\frac{10}{10} - \frac{3}{10} = \frac{7}{10}$. Therefore $\frac{7}{10}$ ordered white coffee. (250 ÷ 10) × 7 = 175

4 **40** The whole amount of 200 = $\frac{5}{5}$ and $\frac{5}{5} - \frac{4}{5} = \frac{1}{5}$. So, $\frac{1}{5}$ of flights are international and $\frac{1}{5}$ of 200 = 40.

5 **10** Add the fractions shown by adding the numerators (top numbers) and leaving the denominators the same: $\frac{1}{13} + \frac{7}{13} = \frac{8}{13}$; $\frac{13}{13}$ = the whole 26 miles, so he walked $\frac{13}{13} - \frac{8}{13} = \frac{5}{13}$. (26 ÷ 13) × 2 = 4

6 **46** minutes 115% means an increase of 15% on top of the original amount. 10% of 40 = 4 minutes and 5% = 2 minutes so 40 + 10 + 5 = 46 minutes.

7 **£32** Refer to Test 2 Q 7 on subtracting fractions and Test 8 Q 3 on finding a fraction of a number. As the fractions are eighths, the whole £64 = $\frac{8}{8}$; $\frac{8}{8} - \frac{1}{8} = \frac{7}{8}$ and $\frac{7}{8} - \frac{3}{8} = \frac{4}{8}$, so Nabeel receives $\frac{4}{8} = \frac{1}{2}$. 64 × $\frac{1}{2}$ = 32.

8 **£24** Refer to Test 8 Q 4 on finding a percentage of a number. £30 × 20 = 600 and 600 ÷ 100 = 6; £30 – £6 = £24.

9–10 Refer to Test 2 Q 5 on multiplying by powers of 10 and Test 1 Q 1 on simplifying fractions.

9 $\mathbf{\frac{1}{5}}$ 1 litre = 1000 ml, so multiply 2.5 l by 1000 to change it into ml = 2500. Therefore, 500 out of 2500 is concentrate, $\frac{500}{2500}$, = $\frac{1}{5}$ when simplified.

10 $\mathbf{\frac{1}{200}}$ 1 kg = 1000 *g*, so multiply 4 kg by 1000 to change it into *g* = 4000. Therefore 20 out of 4000 is fat, which is $\frac{20}{4000} = \frac{1}{200}$ when simplified.

Test 11: Algebra (p 15)

The multiplication sign (×) is not used in algebra: when letters and numbers are placed next to one another, without a +, – × or ÷ sign between them, they need to be multiplied. For example, $2x$ means 2 times x. Also, $1x$ is written as x as the 1 is not usually shown: so, $1y = y$, $1z = z$ and so on. Letters used to represent values can be added, subtracted, multiplied and divided in the same way as numbers: for example, $3a + 2a = 5a$; $6b \times 2 = 12b$; $21p \div 3p = 7p$, $q \times q = q^2$.

1 **16** Write the question as a missing number sentence: [?] × 4 + 12 = 76. Work backwards through the equation completing the inverse (multiply instead of dividing, subtract instead of adding, etc): 76 – 12 = 64; 64 ÷ 4 = 16 (refer to Test 6 Q 4 on short division).

2 **3** The red marbles are represented by x; he has 3 more blue than red, which is $x + 3$; he has 4 times as many green as red, which is $4x$. This gives the equation $x + x + 3 + 4x = 21$ Add each

'x' together to simplify the equation to $6x + 3 = 21$, which is the same as [?] $+ 3 = 21$. $18 + 3 = 21$, so $6x = 18$ and $x = 3$.

3 **6** As it is 3 consecutive numbers, divide 21 by 3 ($21 \div 3 = 7$). Add one and subtract one to the answer to find the consecutive numbers: $7 - 1 = 6$ and $7 + 1 = 8$, so the numbers are 6, 7 and 8.

4 **3** First, add the two amounts of money together: £3.60 + £4.80 = £8.40 (refer to Test 5 Q 5–10 on column addition). Then, divide by 2 to find how much each person has at the end: £8.40 ÷ 2 = £4.20 (refer to Test 6 Q 4 on short division). Subtract this amount from how much Mike originally had: £4.80 – £4.20 = £0.60 (refer to Test 5 Q 10 on column subtraction). £0.60 is the same as 60p which is 3 × 20p coins.

5 **17** $5x = 25$ and $3y = 9$: $25 + 9 = 34$, so $2z = 34$ and $z = 17$.

6 **D** Find the total number of years: $5 + 7 = 12$ years. Akshay's age 5 years ago $= x$, so $12 + x$ is the answer.

7 **D** This equation involves balancing the values (letters and numbers) on each side of the equals sign (=): whatever is done to one side, the same must be done to the other side. The aim is to get a letter on its own on one side of the equals sign and a number on its own on the other. Complete the inverse to balance the sum (refer to Question 1). The equation can be written as $y = \frac{4}{5}x$ (so option A is correct). Begin by getting rid of the fraction by multiplying by 5 on both sides: $y = \frac{4}{5}$ times x so this becomes $5y = 4$ times x. 4 times x is the same as $4x$, so the equation is now $5y = 4x$ (so, option C is correct). Continue balancing by dividing both sides by dividing by 4 to find $\frac{5}{4}y = x$ (so, option B is correct; even if the values are on different sides of the equation sign, it is still the same sum). Return to the original equation and divide both sides by x to get $\frac{y}{x} = \frac{4}{5}$ (so, E is correct). D is the only incorrect option.

8 **$6x$** Draw and label the rectangle to help find the answer: $x + 2x + x + 2x = 6x$.

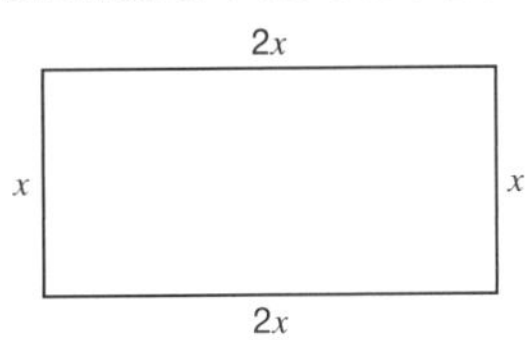

9 **$2x + 7y$** 2 minibuses $= 2x$ and 7 coaches $= 7y$. As the total is being asked for, the sum is addition: $2x + 7y$.

10 **3** Refer to Question 7 on balancing equations. Add 18 to both sides to get $7x + 9 = 10x - 0$ (if you add 9 you will have the sum $7x = 10x - 9$, which will be harder to solve, so sometimes it is best to try both ways on each side and decide which gives the easier sum). $7x + 9 = 10x - 0$ is the same as $7x + 9 = 10x$. Then subtract $7x$ from each side to get $9 = 3x$, so $x = 3$.
When adding and subtracting positive and negative numbers, use a number line. Start at the number you are adding to or subtracting from: count to the right to add and to the left to subtract, for example, $-9 + 18 = 9$ and $-18 + 18 = 0$.

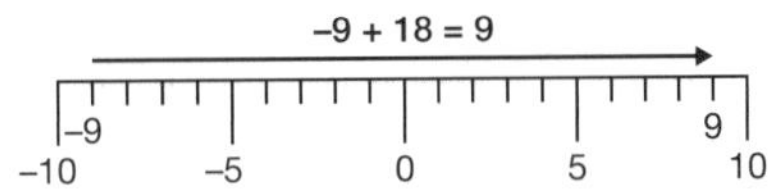

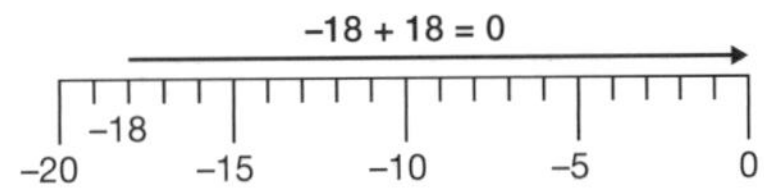

Test 12: Data Handling (pp16–17)

1 **280** The whole pie chart represents 100%, so find the total percentage of the other cars and deduct the answer from 100%: 20% + 25% + 15% = 60% and 100% – 60% = 40%. 100% = 700 cars. Divide by 10 to find 10%: 700 ÷ 10 = 70, so 10% = 70 cars. 40% = 4 × 10% so multiply 70 × 4 to get 280.

2 **12.5 accept 12 or 13** The y-axis is shown as 2 squares going up in intervals of 8 km each time, so, one square is 4 km and 20 km will be half-way between 16 and 24. Use a ruler to draw a line across and mark where the diagonal crosses this line. The x-axis is shown as going up in intervals of 5 each time, so, one square is 2.5 miles. Draw a line down from the point marked on the diagonal: this will be half-way between 10 and 15 miles = 12.5 miles.

3 **22** Add all the numbers together and subtract the answer from 100: 17 + 29 + 13 + 7 + 12 = 78 and 100 – 78 = 22.

4 **A** Look at the box opposite to help decide. The missing option needs to be a question and have the answer of 'YES' if it is a chocolate sweet and 'NO' if it is a mint sweet, therefore 'Is it chocolate?' is the only option that works here.

5 **C** Mark the of co-ordinates on the graph and draw a line to join each pair (refer to Test 1 Q 3 on co-ordinates). Perpendicular lines are at right angles (90°) to one another, so, the answer is C.

6 **2** Add all the numbers together and subtract the answer from 100: 19 + 7 + 4 + 38 + 30 = 98 and 100 – 98 = 2.

7 **D** Refer to Test 4 Qs 6–10 on probability. 8 + 2 + 10 = 20. Red $= \frac{8}{20}$, Green $= \frac{2}{20}$, Black $= \frac{10}{20}$.

8 **135** 12 × 10 = 120 and 3 × 5 = 15. 120 + 15 = 135.

9 **16** Refer to Question 1. 15% + 20% + 40% = 75% and 100% – 75% = 25%. 25% of 64 is 16 (refer to Test 8 Q 4 on finding a percentage of a number). Or, $\frac{1}{4}$ of the pie chart shows children who preferred rowing and $\frac{1}{4}$ of 64 is 16 (refer to Test 8 Qs 3–4 on finding a fraction of a number).

10 **46** Find the total of the matches they won and drew: 7 + 8 + 13 + 2 + 6 + 10 = 46.

Test 13: Number (p 18)

1 **624** Multiply 52 by 12 (refer to Test 7 Q 2 on long multiplication).

2 **13** Use long division to divide 312 by 24. Find how many times 24 goes into 31: only 1 24 goes into 31, so write 1 above and subtract 24 from 31 to find 7. Bring down the 2 from 312 to form the number 72 and use repeated addition to find how many times 24 goes into 72: 24 + 24 + 24 = 72, so write the 3 above.

$$\begin{array}{r} 13 \\ 24\overline{)312} \\ -\,24 \\ \hline 072 \\ -\,72 \\ \hline 0 \end{array}$$

3 **7** Use knowledge of the 3 times table to count up in 30s: 7 × 3 = 21, so 7 × 30 = 210. Therefore 7 complete pieces are made with 10 cm left over.

4 **53** Refer to Question 2 on long division: 2800 ÷ 53 = 52 remainder 44, so 53 coaches are needed.

5 **16** One row and column is added each time, so, the next pattern will show 4 × 4 = 16.

6 **D** A multiple is the result when two numbers are multiplied together: 5 × 7 = 35.

7 **D** Look at the sequence shown in each row: 1 is added each time to the grey tiles; 2 is added to the white tiles; and 3 is added to the total. Continue the sequence for each row: 3 + 1 = 4 grey tiles; 12 + 2 = 14 white tiles; and 15 + 3 = 18 tiles in total.

8 **20** List the factors of 4 and 5, then look for the lowest number in both lists (factors are numbers that can be divided into another number without leaving a remainder). Factors of 4 are 4, 8, 12, 16, 20 and factors of 5 are 5, 10, 15, 20. The answer is 20 as it is the first number to occur in both lists.

9 **24** As 12 is the larger number, use the 12 times table to count up: 1 × 12 = 12, which is not divisible by 8; 2 × 12 = 24, which is divisible by 8 (24 ÷ 8 = 3).

10 **39** Refer to Question 9: 3 × 13 = 39.

Test 14: Algebra (p 19)

1 **3** 4*a* = 4 × 5 = 20; 2*b* = 2 × 2 = 4; 7*c* = 7 × 3 = 21. Rewrite the sum with the numbers: 20 + 4 – 21 = 3.

2 **E** Refer to Test 11 (including Qs 7 and 10 on balancing equations): in option A, both sides of the equation have been doubled; in option B, 3*c* has been subtracted from both sides of the equation; in option C, 20 has been subtracted from both sides; in option D, *c* has been added to each side. However, in option E, 2*b* has been subtracted from one side, but added to the other.

3 **83** Complete the inverse (refer Test 11 Q 1): 168 – 2 = 166; 166 ÷ 2 = 83.

4 **B** The rectangle's width = *x*, so its length = *x* + 8. The perimeter is the total length around the outside, so *x* + *x* + (*x* + 8) +(*x* + 8) = 4*x* + 16. One side of the square = *y*. As a square has 4 equal sides, the perimeter is 4*y*. Subtract to find how much bigger it is: 4*x* + 16 – 4*y*.

5 **1** Refer to Test 11 (including Q 7 and 10 on balancing equations): add 16*x* to both sides so the equation becomes 17 = 3 + 14*x* (write these values on a number line and calculate them in the same way as numbers: –2*x* +16*x* = 14*x*). Then subtract 3 from both sides so it becomes 14 = 14*x*; therefore, *x* = 1.

6 **96** 48 ÷ 3 = 16 (refer to Test 6 Q 4 on short division); 16 × 6 = 96.

7–9 Refer to Test 11 (including Q 7 and 10 on balancing equations).

7 **5** Subtract 2*x* from both sides so the equation becomes *x* + 2 = 7; then subtract 2 from both sides so it becomes *x* = 5.

8 **3** Add *x* to both sides so the equation becomes 32 = 23 + 3*x* (–*x* + *x* = 0); then subtract 23 from both sides so it becomes 9 = 3*x*; therefore, *x* = 3.

9 **6** Write this as an equation to help solve it: she has *x* stamps and if she had 18 more, she would have 4 times as many (4*x*): *x* + 18 = 4*x*; subtract *x* from each side to get 18 = 3*x*; so *x* = 6.

10 **14** Represent the son's age with a letter (*x*). The father is 36 years older, so his age can be written as (*x* + 36) and their total age can be written as (*x*) + (*x* + 36) = 64. Remove the brackets: *x* + *x* + 36 = 64, then simplify to 2*x* + 36 = 64. Subtract 36 from both sides to find the value of 2*x* = 28 therefore, *x* = 14.

Test 15: Shape and Space (pp 20–21)

1–3 When counting along the squares, remember the one that you are 'standing on' does not need to be included.

1 **B** 2 **C** 3 **C**

4 **B** Draw along the diagrams to help find which one is possible: it is only possible on option B.
5 **D** A right angle is 90°.
6 **E** As the circle overlaps the triangle, the lines at the top of the triangle (inside the circle), and the bottom of the triangle are different streets. They form 'crossroads', and in real life, streets either side of a crossroads are separate, so these too can be considered as different streets.

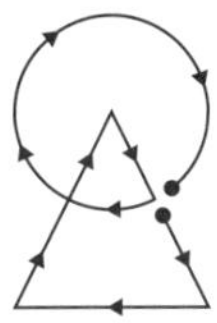

7 **B** A reflex angle is greater than 180°.
8 **150** Each corner of an equilateral triangle is 60° (angles in a triangle always add up to 180° so each angle will be 60° in an equilateral triangle). Each corner of a rectangle is 90° (angles in a quadrilateral always add up to 360°): 60° + 90° = 150°.
9 **70** Refer to Question 8 on angles in a triangle: 180° – 80° – 30° = 70°.
10 **D** A right angle = 90° and angle b is larger, so it cannot be option B. 180° is a straight line and angle b is not larger than an angle on a straight line, so it cannot be A, C or E. Therefore, option D is the closest estimate.

Test 16: Mixed (p 22)

1 **D** In option D, the 2 outside the brackets multiplies everything inside the brackets: 2 times $2x = 4x$ and 2 times $y = 2y$, so $2(2x + y)$ can be simplified to $4x + 2y$.
2 **B** Refer to Test 4 Q 8 on prime numbers and Test 5 Qs 1–4 on square numbers. Only option B shows prime numbers and 17 + 19 = 36, which is 6^2.
3 **18** Refer to Test 13 Q 2 on long division: 435 ÷ 23 = 18 remainder 21.
4 **3** Refer to Test 11 (including Q 7 and 10 on balancing equations). Add x to both sides so the equation becomes $7x + 7 = 28$ $(-x + x = 0)$; then subtract 7 from both sides so it becomes $7x = 21$; so, $x = 3$.
5 **272** 1 hour = 60 minutes and 4 × 60 is 240; 240 + 32 = 272.
6 **C** Use knowledge of the height or length of items you are familiar with, e.g. the height of a door is about 2 metres, so, a man's stride will be approximately 1 metre = 100 cm = 1000 mm. He takes 15 strides, so approximately 1500 cm (100 × 15 = 1500 – refer to Test 2 Q 5 on multiplying by powers of 10). The closest measurement to this is 1400 cm.
7 **B** 5 ham rolls = $5x$ and 3 tuna salads = $3y$. As the total is being asked for, the sum is addition: $5x + 3y$.
8 **Fourteen thousand, two hundred and five** Refer to Test 2 Q 1.
9 **4.32** Refer to Test 2 Qs 7 and 10.
10 **14** Refer to Test 6 Qs 1–4: 7, 9, 14, 21, 22.

Test 17: Mixed (p 23)

1 **13.23** Find the difference between two numbers in the column with the missing value, then add the answer to 11.02: 17.64 – 15.43 = 2.21 and 11.02 + 2.21 = 13.23 (refer to Test 5 Qs 5–10 on column addition and subtraction).
2 **15** Multiply the numbers together to find the answer: 5 × 3 = 15. If 15 is the product of 3 × 5, then it can be divided by 3 and 5 as well.
3 **C** 1 hour = 60 mins and 60 mins × 3 = 180 mins: 10 mins out of 180 is $\frac{10}{180}$ can be simplified to $\frac{1}{18}$ (refer to Test 1 Q 1 on simplifying fractions).
4 **EEE** Refer to Test 3 Q 6 on horizontal symmetry.
5–6 **(2, 12), (8, 3)** Refer to Test 1 Q 3 on co-ordinates.
7 **40** Use times tables knowledge: 8 × 8 = 64, so 64 ÷ 8 = 8; 8 × 5 = 40.
8 **B** Refer to Test 4 Qs 6–10 on probability.
9 **D** Use knowledge of the volume of items you are familiar with, e.g. a large bottle of water is 1.5 litres, so a bucket is the most appropriate answer.
10 **B** 10 mm = 1 cm and 1 cm out of 30 cm is $\frac{1}{30}$.

Test 18: Mixed (pp 24–25)

1 **C** An equilateral triangle has 3 sides of equal length (in this case x) and a square has 4 sides of equal length (in this case y). The question can be written as the length of the wire, $d = 3x + 4y$. It is also true that the perimeters of the two shapes are the same so $3x = 4y$. Substituting this into the first equation, $d = 3x + 3x = 6x$; also $d = 4y + 4y = 8y$. Therefore, statements 1 and 2 are correct. $4x + 3y = d$ is incorrect.
2 **10** List all the multiples of 27 and 37 (refer to Test 13 Q 6 on multiples). Sam pays with £3.00 and Kay pays with £4.00, so look for multiples in each list that have the last two digits the same: these amounts will give the same amount of change. 270 and 370 both end in 70, so, they both received 30p change. 27 × 10 = 270 and 37 × 10 = 370, so they each bought 10.
3 **134** 456 – 322 = 134 (refer to Test 5 Qs 7–8 on column subtraction).
4 **C** Refer to Test 15 Qs 1–3 on completing questions like this.

5 **C** Refer to Test 17 Q 1: 26.25 – 22.97 = 3.28 and 3.28 + 16.40 = 19.68.

6 **22** Refer to Test 12 Q 1. 30% + 15% + 15% = 60% and 100% – 60% = 40%. 100% = 55 households, so divide by 100 to find 1%: 55 ÷ 100 = 0.55 (refer to Test 2 Q 8 on dividing by powers of 10). Multiply the answer by 40 to find 40%: 0.55 × 40 = 22.00. To multiply a decimal number, remove the decimal point and multiply as normal (refer to Test 7 Q 2 on long multiplication): 40 × 55 = 2200. Then count the number of decimal places in the original sum: 40 × 0.55 has 2 digits after the decimal, so, there will be two digits after the decimal in the answer, so 2200 becomes 22.00 = 22.

7 **28** The perimeter of a shape is the total length around the outside: 6 + 9 + 3 + 5 + 5 = 28.

8 **D** Refer to Test 12 Q 2 on using conversion graphs. Find the difference between 130 and 100 on the axis that shows Fahrenheit (F°) = 30. If 3 squares = 30°, then 1 square = 10°. For the axis showing Celsius, find the difference between 0 and 10 = 10. If 2 squares = 10°, then 1 square = 5°.

9 **65** Refer to Test 13 Q 2 on long division: £1300 ÷ 20 = 65.

10 **A** Refer to Test 13 Q 6 on multiples. List all of the multiples of 3 and 5 up to 20 (the highest number shown) to find the answer. Use your knowledge of prime numbers: B and C both contain prime numbers cannot be multiples of 3 or 5.

Test 19: Mixed (p 26)

1 **0.4** When probability is written using decimals, the total of all the possible chances is 1.0, so 0.4 + 0.2 = 0.6 and 1.0 – 0.6 = 0.4.

2 **E** 1 m = 100 cm, so 6 m = 600 cm and 600 + 18 = 618 cm; 618 ÷ 3 = 206.

3 **NOS** Refer to Test 3 Q 4: NOS makes the word SON.

4 $\mathbf{\frac{1}{4}}$ 1 hour = 60 mins and 3 × 60 = 180 mins. 45 mins out of 180 mins is $\frac{45}{180}$, which can be simplified to $\frac{1}{4}$ (refer to Test 1 Q 1 on simplifying fractions).

5 **486** 68 MB + 96 MB = 164 MB and 650 MB – 164 MB = 486 MB (refer to Test 5 Q 5–10 on column addition and subtraction).

6 **E** Draw the reflection onto the diagram using a ruler and protractor.

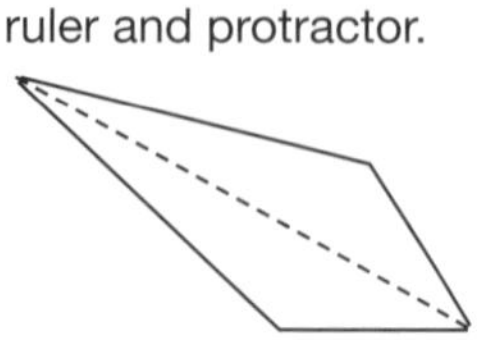

7 **5** Refer to Test 11 (including Questions 7 and 10 on balancing equations): add 2 to each side of the equation so it becomes $4x = 2x + 10$; then subtract $2x$ from each side so it becomes $2x = 10$, so, $x = 5$.

8 **E** 1 litre is approximately the equivalent to 1 kg = 1000 g and 500 g = 0.500 kg = 0.5 kg. 0.500. 1.5 + 1.5 + 3.0 + 0.5 = 6.5 kg

9 **221** 17 × 13 = 221 (refer to Test 7 Q 2 on long multiplication).

10 **29** Refer to Test 11 Q 1: 94 –7 = 87 and 87 ÷ 3 = 29.

Test 20: Mixed (p 27)

1 $\mathbf{\frac{7}{32}}$ Refer to Test 8 Qs 1–4 on converting fractions into decimals to find the smallest: $\frac{1}{4}$ = 0.25, $\frac{3}{8}$ = 0.375, $\frac{2}{5}$ = 0.4, $\frac{2}{7}$ = 0.286 (rounded) and $\frac{7}{32}$ = 0.219 (rounded); therefore $\frac{7}{32}$ is the smallest.

2 $\mathbf{2z}$ $3x$ and $9y$ can be factorised to $3(x + 3y) = 6z$. Divide both sides by 3 to get $x + 3y = 2z$.

3 **J** Copy and cut out the net and assemble it to help find the answer.

4 **B** An obtuse angle is more than 90°, but less than 180°: only B does not have any as it has four right angles (90°).

5 **64** In a ratio, it is important to keep the calculations in the same order: girls to boys = 8 : 9 and the ratio has been changed to [?] : 72. Find how many times 9 has been multiplied by to change it into 72 and multiply the girls by the same number: 9 × 8 = 72 and 8 × 8 = 64.

6 **E** 1 metre = 100 cm, so 2 m = 200 cm; 1 foot is approximately 30 cm. Find how many lots of 30 go into 200. Use knowledge of the 3 times table: if 3 × 6 = 18, then 30 × 6 = 180, so he is 6 feet. Convert the 20 cm remaining (200 – 180 = 20): one inch = 2.5 cm and 8 × 2.5 = 20, so 20 cm = 8 inches. Therefore he is 6 feet 8 inches and option E is closest to this measurement.

7 **P(–2, –3) Q(–3, 2) R(2, –3)** Refer to Test 1 Q 3 on co-ordinates.

8 **£60** Refer to Test 8 Qs 3–4 on finding a fraction of a number: $\frac{7}{7}$ = the whole £420 and $\frac{7}{7} - \frac{6}{7} = \frac{1}{7}$; £420 ÷ 7 = £60.

9 **4** $2y = 14$ and $z = 2$, so the equation can be rewritten as $4x - 14 = 2$. Complete the inverse to solve the sum (refer to Test 11 Q 1): $4x = 2 + 14$, so $4x = 16$ and therefore $x = 4$.

10 **132** Use knowledge of times tables: 11 × 11 = 121, so 121 ÷ 11 = 11; 11 × 12 = 132.

Test 21: Mixed (pp 28–29)

1 **C** The perimeter of a shape is the total length around the outside. Shapes A, B, C and D are all regular shapes, so each of their sides are the same length. A is 10 × 4 = 40; B is 8 × 5 = 40; C is 6 × 6 = 36; and D is 5 × 8 = 40. The opposite sides on the rectangle are the same, so 8 + 8 + 12 + 12 = 40.

2 **C** Draw the reflection onto the diagram using a ruler. An isosceles triangle has 2 sides and 2 angles of the same size.

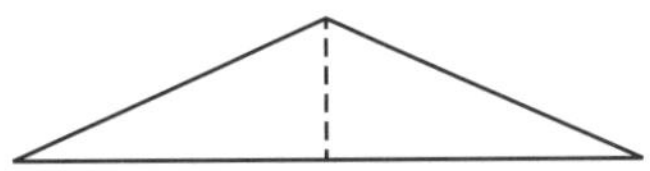

3 **510** 620 + 200 + 200 = 1020 and 1020 ÷ 2 = 510.

4 **B** 1 foot = approximately 30 cm and 30 × 6 = 180 cm; as 100 cm = 1 m, divide 180 by 100 to find 1.8 m (refer to Test 2 Q 8 on dividing by powers of 10).

5 **34 (accept 33)** Refer to Test 12 Q 2 on using conversion graphs. There are 10 increments between 20° and 30°, so, each square along the *x*-axis represents 1°; the number of ice creams sold increases in increments of 5 every 2 squares, so each square represents 2.5 ice creams.

6 **D** Complete the drawing of the shape on the diagram: the shape has 10 sides of equal length, so it is a regular decagon.

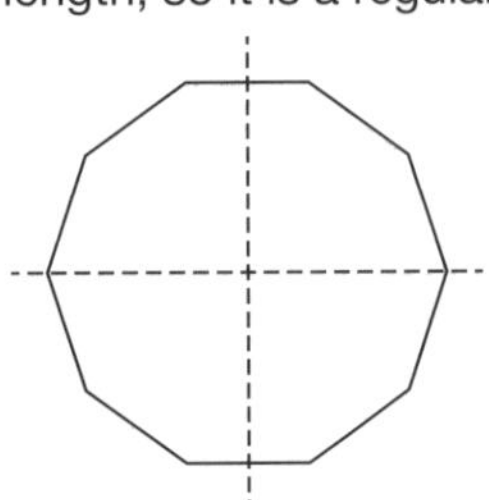

7 **C** Copy and cut out the net shown, then assemble it to find the answer.

8 **30** Separate the shape into 2 triangles and 1 rectangle, then work out the area of each shape (refer to Test 7 Q 4 on finding the area of a rectangle and triangle): 3 × 5 = 15; 15 ÷ 2 = 7.5 (refer to Test 1 Q 3 on short division). Add the answers together to find the total area: 7.5 + 15 + 7.5 = 30

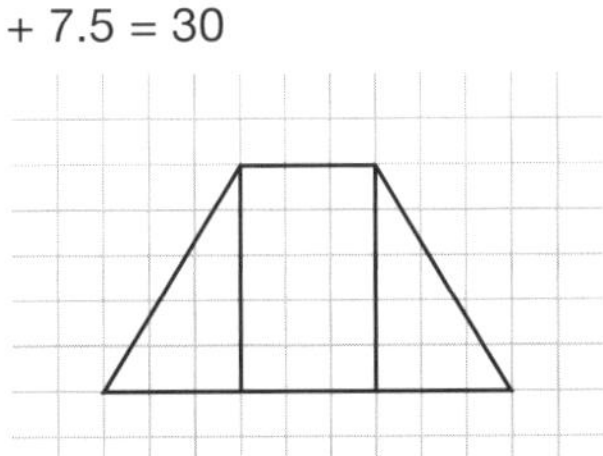

9 **45** The most popular subject is shown by the highest bar: English with 45.

10 **7** £3899 – £700 – £3199; use repeated addition to find how many lots of £457 make 3199 (short and long division will not work easily with this sum): 457 + 457 + 457 + 457 + 457 + 457 + 457 = 3199, i.e., 7 lots of £457 (see Test 5 Qs 5–10 on column addition and subtraction).

Test 22: Mixed (p 30)

1 **B** Use the place value grid shown in Test 2 Q 1.

2 $\frac{2}{3}$ 40 out of 60 minutes is $\frac{40}{60}$ which can be simplified to $\frac{2}{3}$ (refer to Test 1 Q 1 on simplifying fractions).

3 **A** Refer to Test 5 Qs 1–4 on square and cubed numbers: $4^2 = 4 \times 4$ as the '2' represents the number 4 being multiplied twice; $2^3 = 2 \times 2 \times 2$ as the '3' represents the number 2 being multiplied three times. Here 5 is multiplied six times, so the answer is 5^6.

4 **14** Each triangle is the same height and width of each square shown with the dashed lines, so separate each square into triangles as well: a total of 14 triangles are shown.

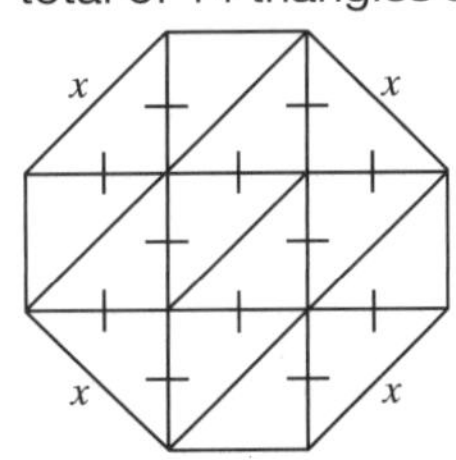

5 **£6.40** Each day: (12 × 4p) + (4 × 20p) = 128p. 128p × 5 days = 640p = £6.40.

6 **HIH** Refer to Test 3 Q 6 on horizontal symmetry.

7 **C** 25p coins do not exist, whereas all the other options show coins that do.

8 **C** The area of a square is found by multiplying the length by the width: as squares have sides of equal length, the length and the width are the same and 8 × 8 = 64. The perimeter is the total length around the outside and 8 × 4 sides = 32.

9 **0.98** Refer to Test 4 Qs 6–10 on probability. As the probability is shown in decimals, subtract 0.02 from 1 using column subtraction (refer to Test 5 Qs 5–10): 1.00 – 0.02 = 0.98.

10 **124** Refer to Test 3 Qs 7–8 on breaking down compound shapes and working out missing measurements: 8 × 6 = 48, 4 × 5 = 20, 7 × 8 = 56. Sum these 48 + 20 + 56 = 124. Or 6 × 4 = 24, 18 × 4 = 72, 4 × 7 = 28 gives 24 + 72 + 28 = 124.

Test 23: Mixed (p31)

1 **600** Use the place value grid shown in Test 2 Q 1.
2 **£19.14** Refer to Test 7 Q 2 on long multiplication: 45p × 34 = 1530p; 32p × 12 = 384p; and 1530 + 384 = 1914p. As 100p = £1.00, divide by 100 (refer to Test 2 Q 8 on dividing by powers of 10): 1914 ÷ 100 = 19.14.
3 **E** A rectangle has two widths of equal length and two sides of equal length, so the total of the lengths is 40 (20 + 20); subtract this from 50 to find the total of both widths: 50 – 40 = 10, so each width is 5 (10 ÷ 2 = 5). Multiply the length by the width to find the area: 5 × 20 = 100.
4 **E** Ratio can be simplified or enlarged by dividing or multiplying both sides by the same number, so, equivalents of 14 : 20 are: 7 : 10 (when divided by 2); 28 : 40 (when multiplied by 2); 2: $\frac{20}{7}$ (when divided by 7 – remember that $\frac{20}{7}$ is the same as 20 ÷ 7); which can be simplified further to 1: $\frac{10}{7}$.Therefore E is the only option that has a different equivalent answer.
5 **C** Refer to Test 15 Q 8 on angles of an equilateral triangle and a quadrilateral: these are both less than 135°, so B and D can be excluded. To find the interior angle of a polygon, first, count the number of sides and subtract 2, then multiply the answer by 180°. Option C has 8 sides: 8 – 2 = 6; 6 × 180° = 1080. Divide the answer by the number of sides to find the size of each interior angle: 1080 ÷ 8 = 135.
6 **16:16** 13:47 + 2 hours = 15:47. As there are 60 minutes in an hour, subtract 47 from 60 to find the amount of minutes until the next hour (16:00): 60 – 47 = 13, then subtract 13 from the 29 minutes to find the amount of remaining minutes that need to be added: 29 – 13 = 16, so the time is 16:16.
7 **C** Count up in lots of 24 as this is the larger number: 2 × 24 = 48 and 4 × 12 = 48.
8 **120** Angles in a quadrilateral always add up to 360° and 90° is often represented with a small square, so: 60 + 90 + 90 = 240; 360 – 240 = 120.
9 **£42.30** Refer to Test 5 Qs 5–10 on column subtraction: 1.64 + 2.12 + 0.89 + 0.20 + 3.45 = 8.30 and 8.30 + 34.00 = 42.30.
10 $\mathbf{\frac{1}{6}}$ Refer to Test 8 Qs 1–4 on converting fractions into decimals: $\frac{2}{3}$ = 0.667 (rounded); $\frac{4}{10}$ = 0.40; $\frac{5}{8}$ = 0.625; $\frac{1}{6}$ = 0.167 (rounded); $\frac{7}{10}$ = 0.70.

Test 24: Mixed (pp32–33)

1 $\mathbf{\frac{5}{7}}$ Refer to Test 8 Qs 1–4 on converting fractions and percentages into decimals: $\frac{5}{7}$ = 0.714; 71% = 0.71; 0.69; $\frac{2}{3}$ = 0.667 (rounded); 65% = 0.65.
2 **37.18** Refer to Test 2 Q 4 on decimals. The number line has 5 increments and the difference between 37.1 and 37. 2 is 0.1, so divide 0.1 by 5 to find how much it goes up by each time: 0.1 ÷ 5 = 0.02. Complete the number line by adding 0.02 to 37.1 onwards: 37.1 + 0.02 = 37.12, 37.12 + 0.02 = 37.14 and so on (refer to Test 5 Qs 5–10 on column addition).
3 **42** The two small lines on either side of the triangle and the word 'isosceles' indicate that those sides (and therefore angles) are the same. All angles in a triangle add up to 180°. 180 – 96 = 84, the total of the two remaining angles; 84 ÷ 2 = 42.
4 **42** Refer to Test 9 Qs 1–2 on volume: 7 × 3 = 21 and 21 × 2 = 42.
5 **16** The ratio is 1 cm : 2 km and 1 cm has been multiplied by 8, so 2 km needs to be multiplied by 8 as well (2 × 8 = 16).
6 **Mr Save** The amounts of money that are owed by people are shown with a '–' sign in front of them: the greatest amount owed shown is £468.
7 **360** To find the area of a triangle, multiply the base by the height and divide by 2: 18 × 40 = 720 and 720 ÷ 2 = 360.
8 **B** Refer to Test 15 Qs 1–3 on completing questions like this.
9 **E** Parallel lines are lines which are always the same distance apart; they never meet or cross. Vertical lines go from top to bottom and horizontal lines go from left to right.
10 **£70** Refer to Test 12 Q 2 on using conversion graphs.

Test 25: Mixed (p34)

1 **0.04** Refer to Test 2 Q 4 on decimals: 0.04 is the same as 0.040.
2 **74** Refer to Test 11 Q 10 on calculating with negative numbers: 0 – 150 = –150 and –150 + 76 = –74; 0 m is sea level, so –74 is 74 m below sea level.
3 **NOOS** Refer to Test 3 Q 3. NOOS makes the word SOON.
4 **E** Refer to Test 8 Qs 1–4 on fractions, decimals and percentages. 0.1, 10% and $\frac{1}{10}$ are all the same amount, so, all give an answer of 2; 10% of 10 is 1, so 20% is 2; 0.01 is the same as 1% and 1% of 20 = 0.2. Also, percentages are

reversible and this can help to make the sum easier: 80% of 5 = 50% of 8 and one of these is easier to calculate than the other.

5 **5** Refer to Test 12 Q 2 on using conversions graphs.

6 **45** Write the question as a missing number sentence: [?] × 2 – 1 = 89. Work backwards through the equation completing the inverse (refer to Test 11 Q 1). 89 + 1 = 90 and 90 ÷ 2 = 45.

7 **1000** Volume = length × width × height. All of these are the same for a cube, so 10 × 10 × 10 = 1000.

8 **B and C** Only a square and rhombus have diagonals that cross at right angles as they are both quadrilaterals with all sides the same length.

9 **102** As 6 is the larger number, use knowledge of times tables to find the first multiple of 6 after 100: 6 × 10 = 60 and 6 × 5 = 30; so 6 × 15 = 90; 90 + 6 = 96 and 96 + 6 = 102. Any number divisible by 6 will be divisible by 3.

10 **60** Jake is travelling in a ratio of 64 : 40, Lee is travelling in a ratio of 32 : 20 and both ratios can be simplified to 16 : 10 and then 8 : 5. Now divide 96 by 8 (using times table knowledge) = 12. The other side of his ratio can be found by multiplying 12 × 5 = 60.

Test 26: Mixed (p 35)

1 **3.2** There are 10 increments between 0 and 2 so each increment is 2 ÷ 10 = 0.2. Complete the number line to find the answer by repeatedly adding 0.2 between 2 and 4: 2.2, 2.4, 2.6 and so on (refer to Test 2 Q 4 on decimals).

2 **180** 72 ÷ 6 = 12 and 12 × 15 = 180. Use long multiplication. Or split into (12 × 10) + (12 × 5) using times table knowledge.

3 **A** Use knowledge of the weight of items you are familiar with, e.g. a mug holds about 250 ml, so, a teaspoon is the most appropriate answer.

4 **D** Refer to Test 7 Q 9 on using factor pairs to find the answer. Factor pairs of 30 are: 1 and 30; 2 and 15; 3 and 10; and 5 and 6. Only 5 + 5 + 6 + 6 gives one of the answers shown (22).

5 **11** Refer to the first diagram on Test 11 Q 10 and use this to count up on: –2 to 9 is 11.

6 **5.99** Refer to Test 2 Qs 7 and 9.

7 **£2793** Round £3.99 to £4.00 to make the sum easier. If 7 × £4 = £28, then 700 × £4 = £2800. 700 lots of 1*p* were added when rounding, so subtract this from 2800: 700*p* = £7 and £2800 – £7 = £2793.

8 **6** A positive number is any number greater than zero. Write the question as a missing number sentence: [?] × [?] ÷ 2 = 18. Work backwards through the equation, completing the inverse (refer to Test 11 Q 1). 18 × 2 = 36 and 6 × 6 = 36.

9 **D** Look at the box opposite to help decide. The missing option needs to be a question and have the answer of 'YES' if it is steel and 'NO' if it is paper, so, 'Is it strong?' is the only option that works.

10 $\mathbf{\frac{6}{7}}$ $\frac{30}{35}$ can be simplified to $\frac{6}{7}$ (refer to Test 1 Q 1).

Test 27: Mixed (pp 36–37)

1 **E** The ratio shown is 1 : 25 000, which means 1 cm = 25 000 cm in real life. 1 cm has been multiplied by 4, so 25 000 needs to be multiplied by 4 as well: if 4 × 25 = 100, then 4 × 25 000 = 100 000. Therefore the ratio becomes 4 : 100 000 and 100 000 cm is the equivalent of 1 km (there are 100 cm in 1 m and 1000 m in 1 km: 100 × 1000 = 100 000 cm).

2 **E** Refer to Test 24 Q 9. Perpendicular lines are at right angles (90°) to one another.

3 **D** Begin by changing 8.27 pm into 24-hour clock by adding 12 to the hours: 8 + 12 = 20, so 8.27 pm is 20:27. Remember that the 24-hour finishes the day at 23:59, then begins the next day at 00:00. Use a number line to count on 6 hours.

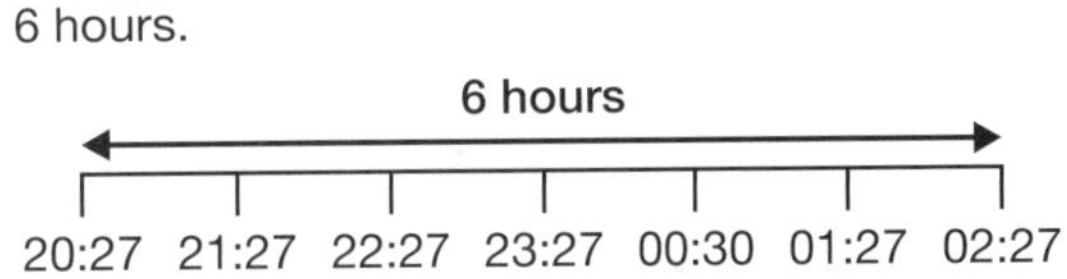

4 **D** Refer to Test 15 Qs 1–3 on completing questions like this.

5 **3.5** If 1000 mA = 1 amp, then 500 mA = 0.5 amp and 4000 mA = 4 amps. The current drops by 500 mA, so 4 amps – 0.5 amp = 3.5 amps.

6 **B** Change the number of hours shown to minutes: there are 60 minutes in 1 hour, so 2 hours = 120 minutes and 3 hours = 180 minutes. Write these calculations as the denominator (bottom number) and the number of minutes shown as the numerator (top number). A = $\frac{30}{120}$, B = $\frac{20}{180}$, C = $\frac{15}{120}$, D = $\frac{40}{60}$ and E = $\frac{10}{60}$. Next, convert the fractions so they have the same denominator. 180 is the largest denominator, so count up in lots of 180: 180 × 2 = 360; 120 and 60 also go into 360. Remember to multiply the numerator and denominator by the same number: e.g. 120 × 3 = 360, so the numerators need to be multiplied by 3 as well. A = $\frac{90}{360}$, B = $\frac{40}{360}$, C = $\frac{45}{360}$, D = $\frac{240}{360}$ and E = $\frac{60}{360}$.

7 **B** The top two corners are right angles, as the arrows indicate parallel lines, so, they are 90° each. Angle c is obtuse (more than 90°, but less than 180°), so the answer must be option A or B. The size of the angle is slightly larger than 90°, so B is the most appropriate answer.

8 **16** $12 \times 8 = 96$: this means 96 grooves on the first cog have rotated, so find how many lots of 6 are in 96 to find how many revolutions the smaller cog makes; $96 \div 6 = 16$.

9 **63** $27 \times 7 = 189$ and $189 \div 3 = 63$.

10 **2** 50% is equivalent to $\frac{1}{2}$ (refer to Test 1 Q 1). The shape has been separated into sixths and $\frac{1}{6}$ is already shaded: 2 more triangles need to be shaded to make $\frac{1}{2}$ (50%).

Test 28: Mixed (p38)

1 **26** Add all the numbers together and subtract the total from 100: $3 + 12 + 23 + 18 + 18 = 74$ and $100 - 74 = 26$.

2 **12** A positive number is any number to the right of the zero on a number line (refer to the first diagram shown in Test 11 Q 10). Use knowledge of times tables: $12 \times 12 = 144$.

3 **£350000** Divide 14000 by 1000 to simplify the sum: $14 \times 25 = 350$. Then multiply the answer by 1000 to return it to its original form: $350 \times 1000 = 350000$ (see Test 7 Q 2 on long multiplication and Test 2 Qs 5 and 8 on multiplying and dividing by powers of 10).

4 **135** The difference between each adjacent number is 13 and each row and column has the following numbers: 109, 135 and 148.

5 **63%** Refer to Test 1 Q 1 on simplifying fractions and Test 8 Qs 5–7 on converting fractions into percentages: As a percentage, 378 out of 600 is $\frac{378}{600} \times 100 = \frac{378}{6}$. Use short division to find 63%.

6 **11** Add all the numbers together and subtract the total from 100: $13 + 1 + 18 + 54 + 3 = 89$ and $100 - 89 = 11$.

7 **0.036** Refer to Test 9 Qs 1–2 on volume and Test 18 Q 6 on multiplying decimals: $2 \times 6 \times 3 = 36$. There are 3 decimal places in the sum $0.2 \times 0.6 \times 0.3$, so there will be 3 decimal places in the answer, so it becomes 0.036.

8 **C** An edge is where two faces meet and shape D has 12 edges: $12 - 3 = 9$ and only option C has 9 edges.

9 **195** Find 10% by dividing by 10, then multiply the answer by 3 to find 30%: $150 \div 10 = 15$ and $15 \times 3 = 45$. Add 45 to 150 g to find the answer: $45 + 150 = 195$.

10 **4*p*** Refer to Test 11 (including Qs 7 and 10 on balancing equations). The equation is $p = \frac{3}{4}q$ ($\frac{3}{4}$ of q is the same as $3 \div 4$ times q). Multiply both sides of the equation by 4 to change it to $4p = 3q$.

Test 29: Mixed (p39)

1 **50000** Refer to the diagrams on Test 11 Q 10 on negative numbers. As negative numbers 'mirror' positive numbers, −67 is the lowest temperature shown, therefore the coldest.

2 **B** Refer to Test 24 Q 3: $47 + 47 = 94$ and $180 - 94 = 86$.

3 $\mathbf{\frac{4}{5}}$ 40 out of 50 is $\frac{40}{50}$ and can be simplified to $\frac{4}{5}$ (refer to Test 1 Q 1).

4 **B** Refer to Test 6 on range: $197 - 171 = 26$.

5 **50*x* + 20*y*** The boxes of pencils = $50x$ and the boxes of pens = $20y$. The question is asking how many she orders altogether, so the sum is addition: $50x + 20y$.

6 **6.63** Refer to Test 2 Q 4 on decimals. The number line has 5 increments between 6.55 and 6.65, so divide (6.65×6.55) by 5 to find the value of each increment (= 0.02) (refer to Test 1 Q 3 on short division). Complete the number line by adding 0.02 to 6.55 onwards: $6.55 + 0.02 = 6.57$, $6.57 + 0.02 = 6.59$ and so on (refer to Test 5 Qs 5–10 on column addition).

7 **16** Refer to Test 13 Q 2 on long division: $293 \div 18 = 16$ remainder 5, so 16 complete packets.

8 **D** Both sides of the ratio need to be divided by or multiplied by the same number to find an equivalent ratio: only 5 : 1 cannot do this.

9 **15** Refer to Test 5 Qs 1–4 on square and cubed numbers.

10 **116 or 117** Subtract to find the answer: $1453 - 1337 = 116$, but the year the war began needs to be included too, so 116 + 1 year = 117. However, either answer is acceptable.

Test 30: Mixed (pp40–41)

1 ***y* + 15** Find the total number of years: $13 + 2 = 15$ years. Stu's age 13 years ago = y, so $y + 15$ is the answer.

2 **Thursday** The least amount of loaves were sold on Thursday (5 rolls).

3 **144** Refer to Test 8 Qs 3–4 on finding a fraction of a number: $360 \div 5 = 72$, so $\frac{1}{5} = 72$ and $\frac{2}{5} = 144$. $360 - 72 = 288$ and $288 - 144 = 144$ (refer to Test 5 Qs 5–10 on column subtraction).

4 **A** Refer to Test 1 Q 3 on co-ordinates.

5 **210** Refer to Test 12 Q 1.14% + 12% + 46% = 72%, and 100% − 72% = 28%. 100% =

750 people, so divide by 100 to find 1%: 750 ÷ 100 = 7.5, so 1% = 7.5 people and 7.5 × 28 = 210 (refer to Test 2 Q 8 on dividing by powers of 10 Test 18 Q 6 on multiplying decimals).

6 **45** Find the total of matches they drew and lost: 4 + 6 + 8 = 18; 12 + 8 + 7 = 27; and 18 + 27 = 45.

7 **38** Begin with the first column: 58 + 19 = 77 and 117 – 77 = 40. Then complete the top two rows: 40 + 18 = 58 and 117 – 58 = 59; 58 + 20 = 78 and 117 – 78 = 39. Finally, complete the last two columns: 18 + 39 = 57 and 117 – 57 = 60; 59 + 20 = 79 and 117 – 79 = 38. Check by calculating the bottom row: 19 + 60 = 79 and 117 – 79 = 38.

8 **15** Refer to Test 12 Q 2 on using conversion graphs: the temperature is increasing in increments of 1°C; the number of ice creams is going up in increments of 5 every 2 squares.

9 $\frac{1}{2}$ or 0.5 or 50% Refer to Test Qs 6–10 on probability. There are 8 possible outcomes and a total of 4 odd numbers, i.e., $\frac{4}{8}$ and can be simplified to $\frac{1}{2}$ (refer to Test 1 Q 1). 0.5 or 50% is also acceptable as they are both equivalents of $\frac{1}{2}$.

10 **E** Look at the box opposite to help decide. The missing option needs to be a question about the type of car, with the answer of 'YES' if it is a blue saloon and 'NO' if it is a blue sports car. Therefore 'Is it a saloon?' is the only option that works here.

Puzzle 1 (page 42)

204

a **8 different sizes** There are 8 rows and columns, therefore 8 different sizes.

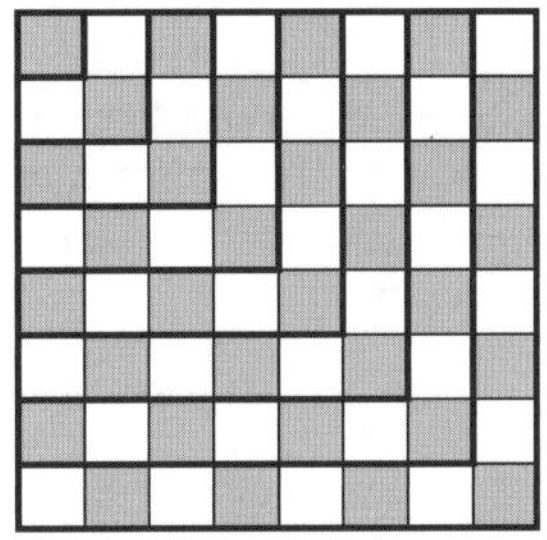

b **8 × 8 = 64 of the 1 by 1 squares**

c **1 × 1 = 1 of the 8 × 8 squares**
2 × 2 = 4 of the 7 by 7 squares
3 × 3 = 9 of the 6 by 6 squares
4 × 4 = 16 of the 5 by 5 squares
5 × 5 = 25 of the 4 by 4 squares
6 × 6 = 36 of the 3 by 3 squares
7 × 7 = 49 of the 2 by 2 squares
1 + 4 + 9 + 16 + 25 + 36 + 49 = 140

Puzzle 2 (page 43)

a **1, 4, 9, 16, 25**
Complete a table to keep a tally of the lights going on and off. The first few are shown below.

Care-taker	Office 1	Office 2	Office 3	Office 4	Office 5	Office 6	Office 7	Office 8	Office 9	Office 10	Office 11	Office 12
1	OFF	OFF	OFF	OFF	OFF	OFF	OFF	OFF	OFF	OFF	OFF	OFF
2		ON		ON		ON		ON		ON		ON
3			ON			OFF			ON			OFF
4				OFF				OFF				ON

b Square numbers Refer to Test 5 Qs 1–4 on square numbers.

Puzzle 3 (page 44)

	1	2		5	5	
5		3	6		2	7
6	5		6	1		7
	8	7		9	1	
4		4	3		4	9
2	9		8	3		2
	6	7		4	8	

Refer to: Test 5 Qs 1–4 on square and cubed numbers; Test 13 Q 6 on multiples; Test 4 Q 7 on prime numbers.

Across

1 A dozen is twelve.
3 110 ÷ 2 = 55
6 $6^2 = 6 \times 6 = 36$
8 $3^3 = 3 \times 3 \times 3 = 27$
10 5 × 13 = 65
12 $5^2 = 25$ and $6^2 = 36$: 25 + 36 = 61
14 $7^2 = 49$: 36 + 49 + 2 = 87
16 102 – 11 = 91
19 37 + 6 = 43
21 $7^2 = 49$
23 $2^2 = 4$ and $5^2 = 25$: 4 + 25 = 29
25 100 – 17 = 83
27 60 + 7 = 67
28 51 – 3 = 48

Down

2 23
4 23 + 29 = 52
5 7 × 8 = 56
7 6 × 11 = 66
9 7 × 11 = 77, so 77 is divisible by 7 and 11 as well.
11 79 – 21 = 58
13 1 × 19 = 19
15 2 × 37 = 74
17 14lbs = 1 stone
18 2 × 21 = 42
20 2 × 19 = 38
22 4 × 23 = 92
24 $10^2 - 2^2 = 100 - 4 = 96$
26 2 × 17 = 34, therefore 34 is divisible by 17, 34 ÷ 17 = 2

Puzzle 4 (page 45)

 = 5  = 8  =9

Row totals: **30**, 27, **31**, 26

Column totals: **34**, 20, **30**, **30**

Begin with the column showing 4 dogs = 20: 20 ÷ 4 = 5, so each dog represents 5. The bottom row shows 2 dogs and 2 cats, so work this one out next: 2 dogs = 10 and 26 – 10 = 16. Therefore if 2 cats = 16, 1 cat = 8. Then work out the second row: 5 + 8 + 5 = 18, so subtract this from 27 to find the number the owl represents (27 – 18 = 9). Use this information to work out the rest of the missing numbers.

Puzzle 5 (page 46)

1 kg, 2 kg, 4 kg, 8 kg, 16 kg

Create a table to keep tally. A 1 kg weight is needed to make 1 kg, so Box 1 is 1 kg. The only way 2 kg can be made is with 2 × 1 kg weights or 1 × 2 kg weight: as the boxes cannot be the same weight, Box 2 must be 2 kg. Boxes 1 and 2 can then be used to make 3 kg. The only way to make 4 kg is with 2 × 2 kg or 1 kg + 3 kg, however, there is only one of each weight and no 3 kg weight to use, so Box 3 must be 4 kg. 5 kg can then be made using Boxes 1 and 3 (1 kg + 4 kg = 5 kg), 6 kg can be made using Boxes 2 and 3 (2 kg + 4 kg) and so on. The beginning of the table is shown on the right: continue the pattern until 31 kg is reached.

Weight	Weights used
1 kg	1 kg
2 kg	2 kg
3 kg	1 kg + 2 kg
4 kg	4 kg
5 kg	1 kg + 4 kg
6 kg	2 kg + 4 kg
7 kg	1 kg + 2 kg + 4 kg
8 kg	8kg
9 kg	1 kg + 8 kg
10 kg	2 kg + 8 kg
11 kg	1 kg + 2 kg + 8 kg
12 kg	4 kg + 8 kg
13 kg	1 kg + 4 kg + 8 kg
14 kg	2 kg + 4 kg + 8 kg
15 kg	1 kg + 2 kg + 4 kg + 8 kg
16 kg	16 kg

5

Here is part of a conversion table. Which figure is missing from the table?

ft	m
5	1.53
6	1.83
7	2.13
8	2.44

m	ft
5	16.40
6	?
7	22.97
8	26.25

Circle the answer.

A 18.23 ft

B 19.01 ft

C 19.68 ft

D 15.33 ft

E 16.40 ft

6

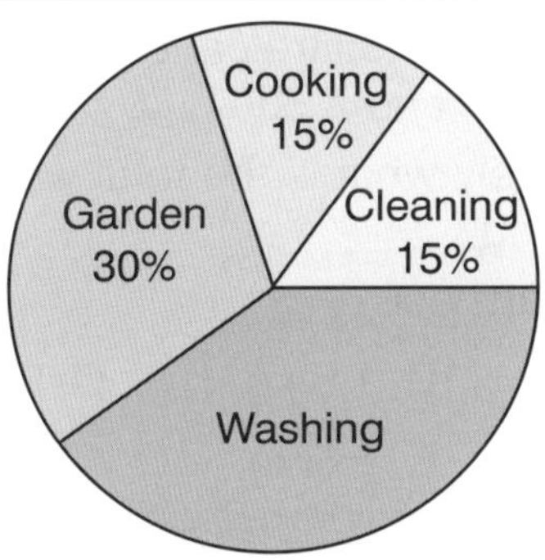

Of 55 households surveyed, how many used most of their water for washing?

____

7

What is the perimeter of the room?

____________ m

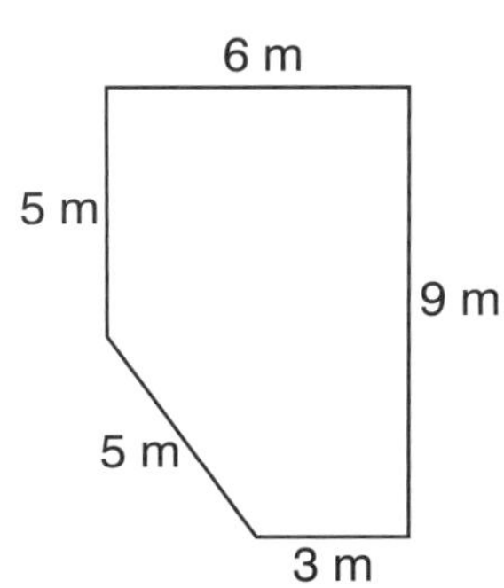

8

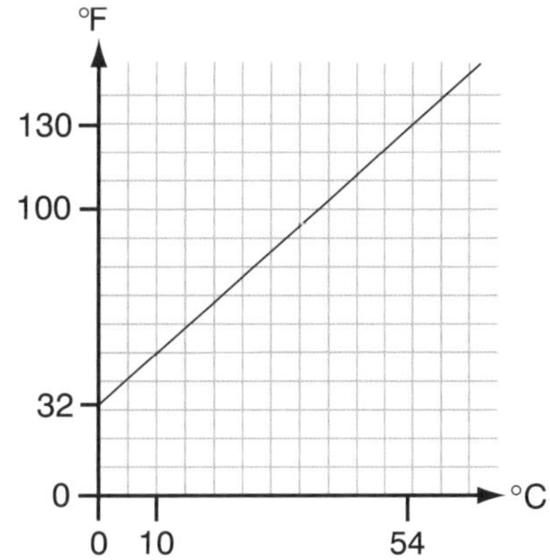

Look at the graph to show the temperature conversion between Fahrenheit (°F) and Celsius (°C).

Use your graph to work out how many degrees Fahrenheit are equivalent to 30° Celsius.

Circle the answer.

A 0 **B** 90 **C** 80 **D** 86 **E** 76

9

Iris withdraws £1300 from her bank account.

She is given the money in £20 notes.

How many £20 notes does she have in total?

____

10

Which circle contains only multiples of either 3 or 5?

Circle the answer.

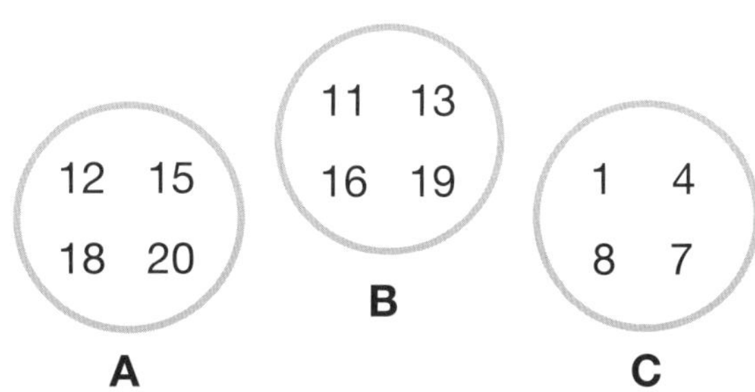

Time for a break! Go to Puzzle Page 44

Total

Test 19: **Mixed**

Test time: 0 5 10 minutes

1

The probability that Mr Yang will catch the bus to school is 0.4.

The probability he will walk is 0.2.

Otherwise he will drive to school.

What is the chance that he will drive to school?

____

2

A piece of wood 6 m 18 cm long is to be cut into three equal pieces.

How long will each piece be?

Circle the answer.

A 3 m 6 cm **B** 2 m 60 cm **C** 3 m 0.6 cm

D 306 m **E** 206 cm

3

NOZ ONS NSO ZNO NOS

Which of these makes a word when rotated through 180°?

Circle the correct word.

4

What fraction of 3 hours is 45 minutes?

____

5

Jen wants to save two files onto a USB stick.

One file is 68 MB. The other is 96 MB.

A USB stick can hold 650 MB.

How many MB of space will be left on the USB stick once she has saved both files?

____

6

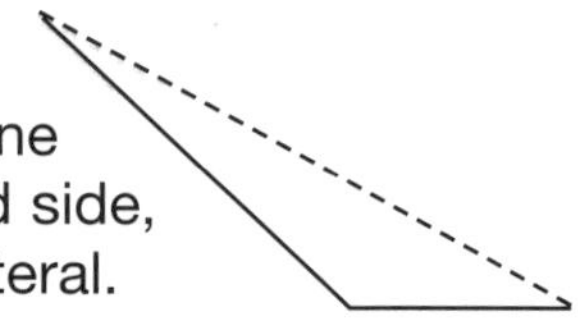

Reflecting this scalene triangle in its dashed side, will make a quadrilateral.

What is the name of this quadrilateral?

Circle the answer.

A Square **B** Rectangle **C** Rhombus

D Parallelogram **E** Kite

7

If $4x - 2 = 2x + 8$, what is the value of x?

____

8

Daxa buys two 1.5 litre cartons of juice, 3 litres of milk and a 500 g jar of coffee.

Approximately what is the total weight of the shopping?

Circle the answer.

A 0.5 kg **B** 1.5 kg **C** 2.5 kg

D 5.5 kg **E** 6.5 kg

9

Amanda plants 17 rows and 13 columns of cabbage plants in a rectangular pattern.

How many cabbage plants has she planted altogether?

____

10

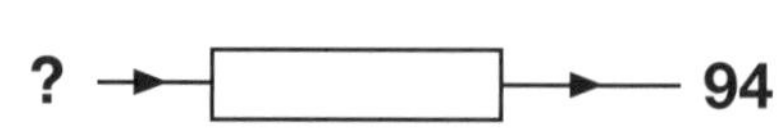

This machine triples and then adds 7.

Which number has been put in?

____

Total

Test 20: Mixed

Test time: 0 5 10 minutes

1 $\frac{1}{4}$ $\frac{3}{8}$ $\frac{2}{5}$ $\frac{2}{7}$ $\frac{7}{32}$

Which of these fractions has the lowest value?

Circle the answer.

2

Given that $3x + 9y = 6z$,

what is the value of $x + 3y = ?$

Give the answer in terms of z.

____

3

When the net is folded to make the cuboid, which corner will join to corner L?

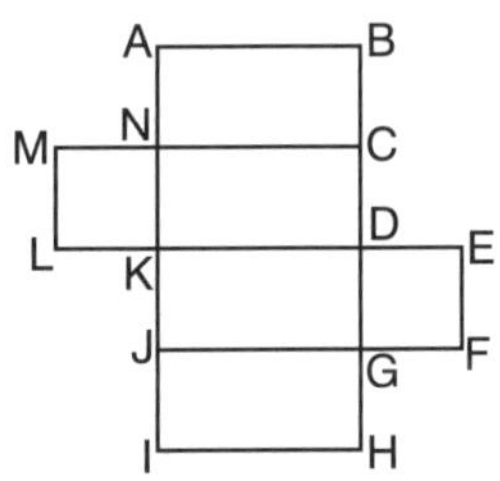

____

4

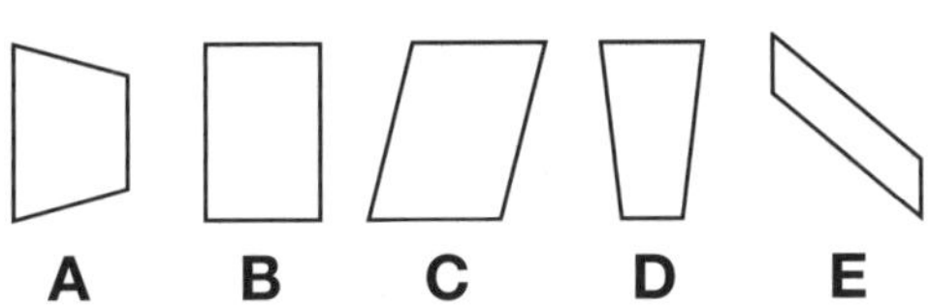

Which quadrilateral does not have an obtuse angle?

Circle the answer.

5

In Grange School, girls and boys are in the ratio 8 : 9.

There are 72 boys, how many girls are there?

____

6

Norbert is 2 metres 0 centimetres tall.

Which is the closest to his height in feet and inches?

Circle the answer.

A 5 feet 11 inches **B** 6 feet 1 inch

C 6 feet 3 inches **D** 6 feet 5 inches

E 6 feet 7 inches

7

Find the coordinates of points P, Q and R.

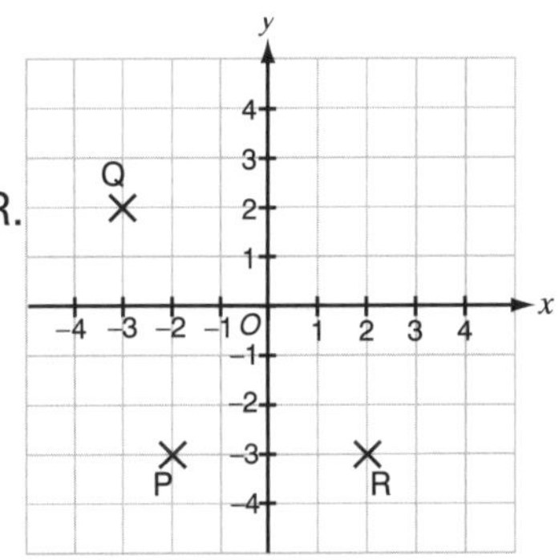

P (___, ___)

Q (___, ___)

R (___, ___)

8

£420 is raised at a Funday.

$\frac{6}{7}$ of the money is donated to charity.

The rest is kept as profit.

How much profit is made?

____

9 $4x - 2y = z.$

Find the value of x when $y = 7$ and $z = 2$.

____

10 121 → [÷11] → [×12] → ________

Complete the function machine.

Total

TEST 21: **Mixed**

Test time: 0 5 10 minutes

1

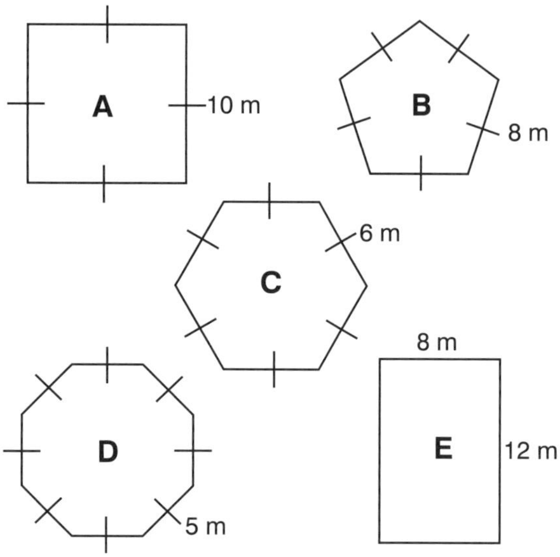

Which shape has a different perimeter from the others?

____

2

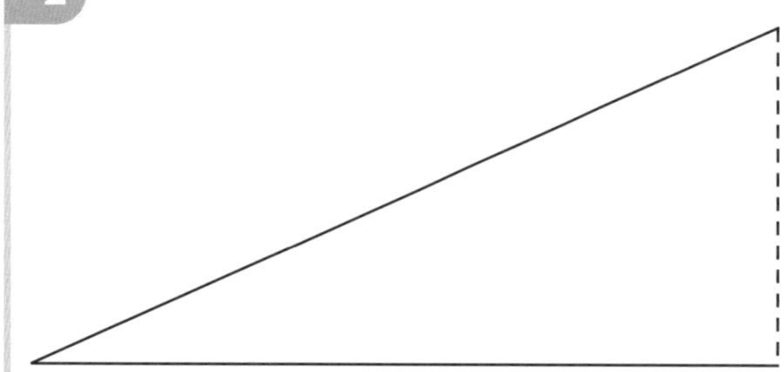

Reflecting this right-angled triangle in its dashed side will make another triangle.

What is the name of this triangle?

Circle the answer.

A Equilateral

B Scalene

C Isosceles

D Right-angled

E Regular

3

Lauren was carrying a 620 g bag of potatoes, and two 200 g bags of fruit.

The total weight of Peter's bags was exactly half the total weight of Lauren's bags.

How much weight did Peter carry?

________ g

4

Miss Drake is 6 feet 0 inches tall.

Which is the closest to her height in metres?

Circle the answer.

A 1.7 m **B** 1.8 m **C** 1.9 m

D 2.0 m **E** 2.1 m

5

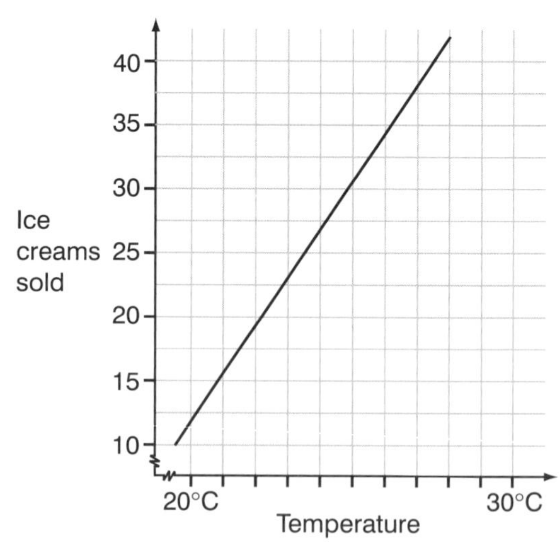

How many ice creams were sold when the temperature was 26°C?

____

6

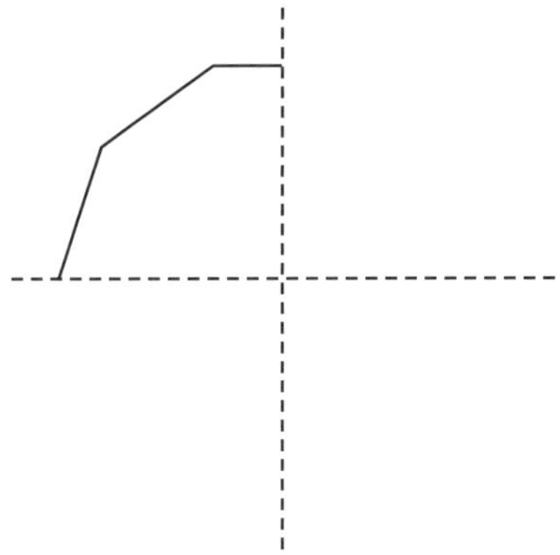

The diagram shows part of a shape and two lines of symmetry.

What is the name of the complete shape?

Circle the answer.

A Regular hexagon

B Regular octagon

C Regular dodecagon

D Regular decagon

E Irregular dodecagon

7

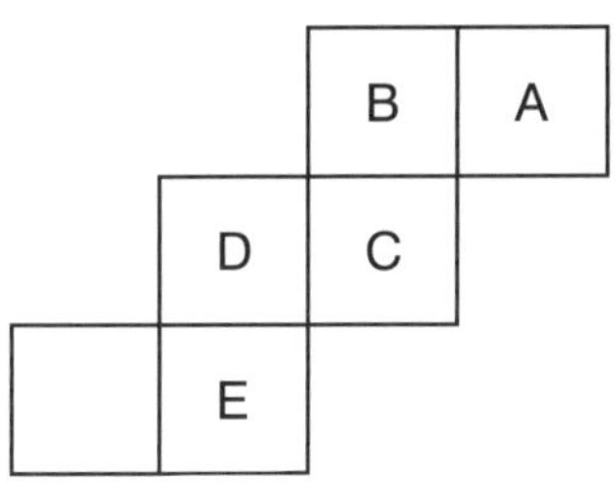

Look at this net of a closed cube.

Which side will be directly opposite the unmarked side, when it is folded to make the cube?

Circle the answer.

A **B** **C** **D** **E**

8

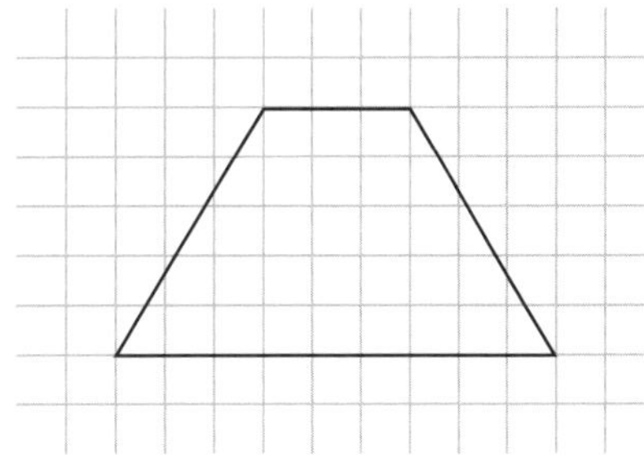

In the diagram above 1 square represents 1 cm^2.

What is the area of the trapezium?

_________ cm^2

9

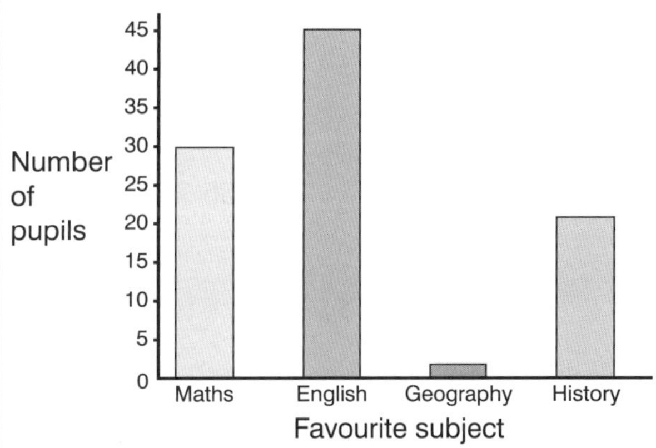

How many people like the most popular subject?

____

10

May pays a £700 deposit towards a car costing £3899.

She saves £457 per month toward the total cost.

How many months does it take her to save the rest of the money?

____

Total

TEST 22: **Mixed**

Test time: 0 5 10 minutes

1

In which number is the 7 worth seven hundred?

Circle the answer.

A 70 608 **B** 83 768 **C** 1127

D 103 872 **E** 47 316

2

What fraction of 1 hour is 40 minutes?

Leave your answer in its simplest form.

____

3

$5 \times 5 \times 5 \times 5 \times 5 \times 5 = ?$

Circle the answer.

A 5^6 **B** 30 **C** 6^5 **D** 555 555 **E** 56

4

The sides labelled x are the same length.

How many times will the small right-angled triangle fit into the octagon?

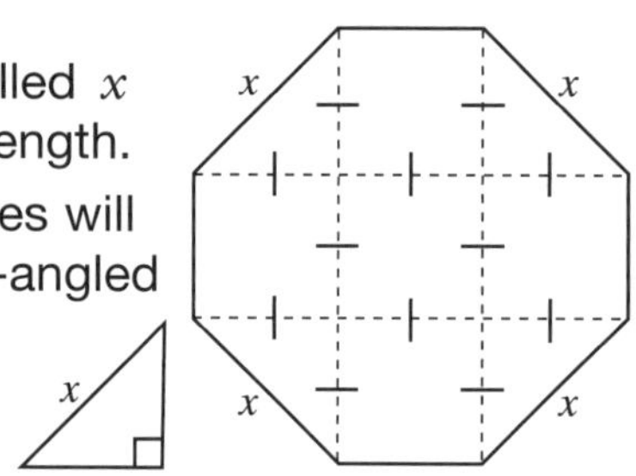

____

5

Ian sends 12 text messages daily costing 4p each.

He makes 4 calls each day costing 20p each.

How much does he spend altogether over five days?

____

6

Which of these has a horizontal line of symmetry?

Circle the answer.

HIM **MIM** **TIM** **LIN** **HIH**

7

Cindy has to pay £1 to enter a fair.

She only has one type of coin.

Circle the option which she could not use.

A One £1 coin **B** Two 50p coins

C Four 25p coins **D** Five 20p coins

E Ten 10p coins

8

The area of a square is 64 cm^2.

What is the perimeter of the square?

Circle the answer.

A 16 cm **B** 9 cm **C** 32 cm

D 50 cm **E** 64 cm

9

The probability it will snow on Christmas Day 2020 is 0.02.

What is the chance it will not snow on Christmas Day 2020?

____

10

What is the area of the shape?

________ m^2

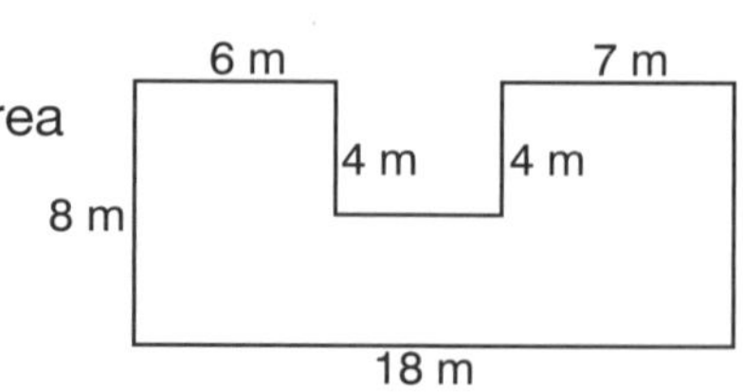

Total

Test 23: **Mixed**

Test time: 0 5 10 minutes

1

What is the six in the number 7608 worth?

____

2

Una sells ice lollies for 45p and ice cream cones for 32p.

She sells 34 of the ice lollies and 12 cones.

How much does she make altogether?

£________

3 The perimeter of a rectangle is 50 cm. If the rectangle is 20 cm long, what is the area of the rectangle?

Circle the answer.

A 40 cm^2 **B** 70 cm^2 **C** 60 cm^2

D 250 cm^2 **E** 100 cm^2

4

Which ratio is not the same as the ratio 14 : 20?

Circle the answer.

A 7 : 10 **B** $2 : \frac{20}{7}$ **C** $1 : \frac{10}{7}$

D 28 : 40 **E** 10 : 16

5

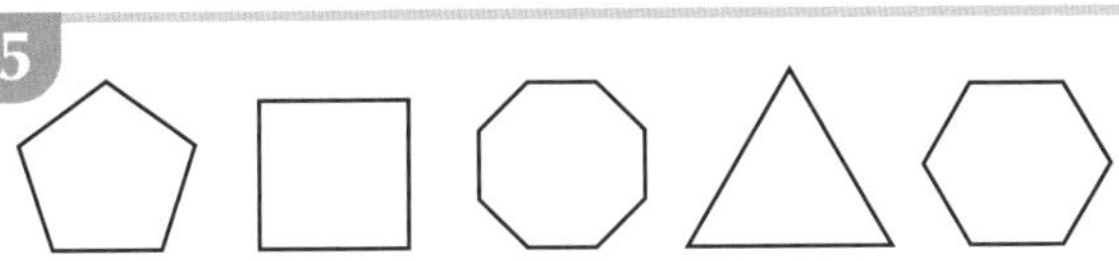

A **B** **C** **D** **E**

An angle inside a polygon is called an interior angle.

Which one of the above regular polygons has an interior angle of 135°?

Circle the answer.

6

A train leaves London at 13.47. The journey to Leeds takes 2 hours and 29 minutes.

What time does it arrive in Leeds?

____

7

Which number is divisible by 12 and 24?

Circle the answer.

A 12 **B** 36 **C** 48 **D** 60 **E** 80

8

Find the size of the unmarked angle.

________ °

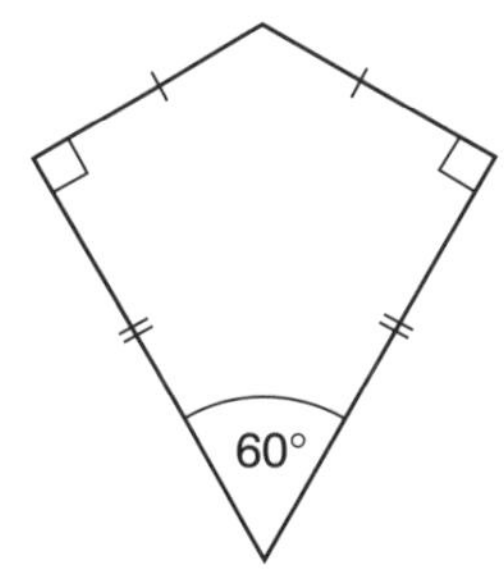

9

Jennie collected money for a charity.

One morning she received the following donations:

£1.64 £2.12 £0.89 20p £3.45

She collected £34 in the afternoon.

How much did she collect in total?

____

10

Which of the following fractions has the smallest value?

Circle the answer.

$\frac{2}{3}$ $\frac{4}{10}$ $\frac{5}{8}$ $\frac{1}{6}$ $\frac{7}{10}$

Total

TEST 24: **Mixed**

Test time: 0 5 10 minutes

1

Which of the following has the largest value?

Circle the answer.

$\frac{5}{7}$ 71%   0.69 $\frac{2}{3}$ 65%

2

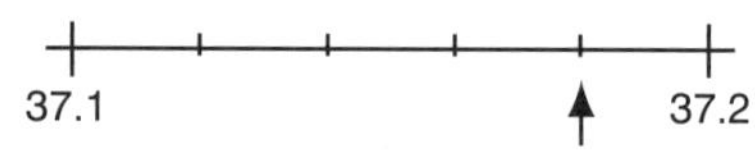

What number does the arrow point to?

____

3

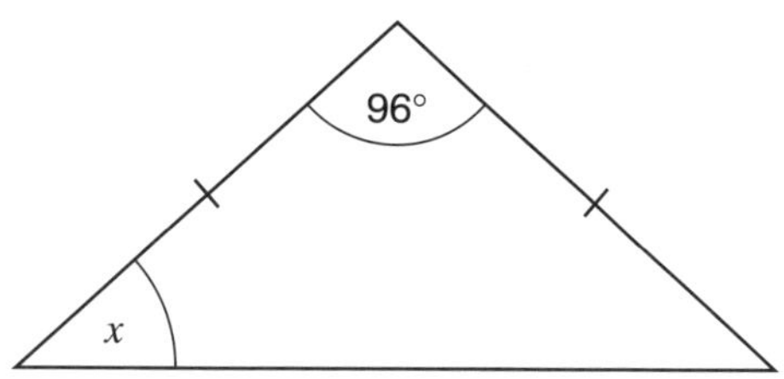

Find the size of the angle marked x in this isosceles triangle.

________ °

4

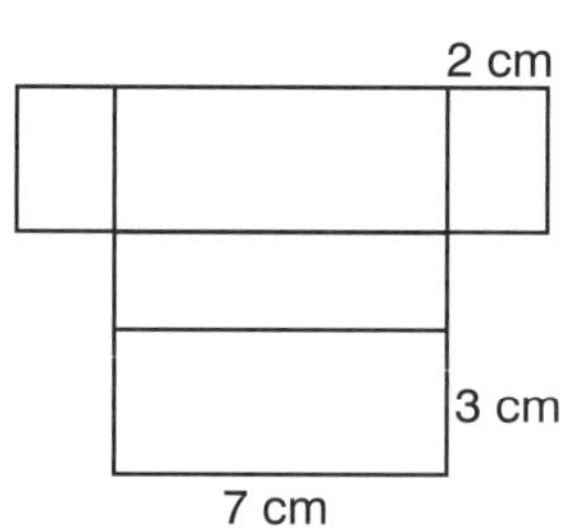

This is a net of an open cuboid.

It is then folded to make an open box.

What is the volume of the box?

__________ cm^3

5

Mike is using a map where 1 cm represents 2 km.

His walk is 8 cm on the map.

How far will his actual walk be?

________ km

6

Name	*Bank Balance*
Mr Spend	–£145
Mr Save	–£468
Mr Broke	£12
Mr Rich	£567
Mr Debt	–£222
Miss Out	£879

The table above shows the balance of six people's bank accounts.

Who owes the most money?

____

7

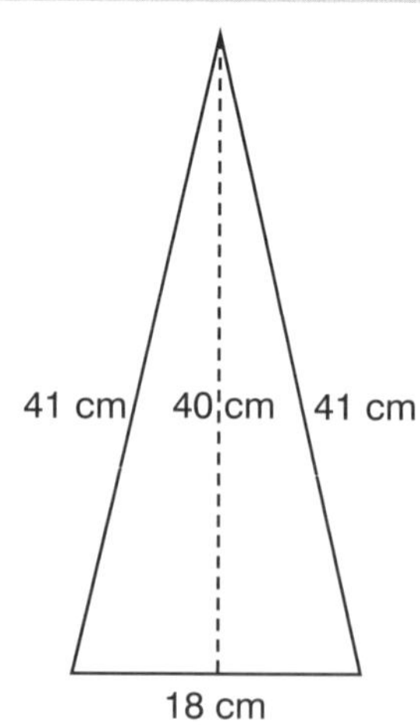

What is the area of the triangle?

________ cm^2

8

Guide the car along the white squares on the plan from the start to the finish.

It can only move FORWARD, TURN RIGHT 90° and TURN LEFT 90°.

Circle the correct instructions.

A FORWARD 3, TURN LEFT 90°, FORWARD 3, TURN LEFT 90°, FORWARD 2, TURN LEFT 90°, FORWARD 4, TURN RIGHT 90°, FORWARD 2, TURN RIGHT 90°, FORWARD 2, TURN LEFT 90°, FORWARD 1

B FORWARD 3, TURN RIGHT 90°, FORWARD 2, TURN LEFT 90°, FORWARD 2, TURN LEFT 90°, FORWARD 4, TURN RIGHT 90°, FORWARD 2, TURN RIGHT 90°, FORWARD 2, TURN LEFT 90°, FORWARD 1

C FORWARD 3, TURN LEFT 90°, FORWARD 3, TURN LEFT 90°, FORWARD 2, TURN LEFT 90°, FORWARD 4, TURN LEFT 90°, FORWARD 2, TURN RIGHT 90°, FORWARD 3, TURN LEFT 90°, FORWARD 1

D FORWARD 3, TURN RIGHT 90°, FORWARD 2, TURN LEFT 90°, FORWARD 2, TURN LEFT 90°, FORWARD 4, TURN RIGHT 90°, FORWARD 2, TURN RIGHT 90°, FORWARD 3, TURN RIGHT 90°, FORWARD 1

E FORWARD 3, TURN RIGHT 90°, FORWARD 2, TURN LEFT 90°, FORWARD 2, TURN LEFT 90°, FORWARD 4, TURN RIGHT 90°, FORWARD 2, TURN LEFT 90°, FORWARD 2, TURN RIGHT 90°, FORWARD 1

9

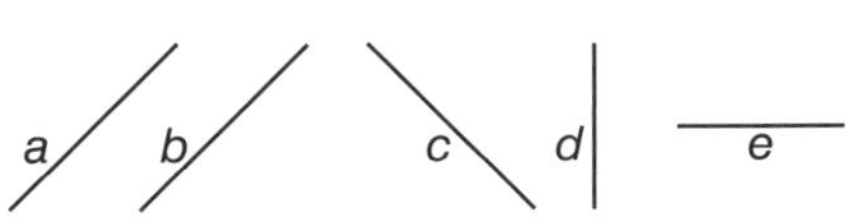

Which of the statements is correct?

Circle the answer.

A *b* and *c* are parallel

B *a* and *b* are vertical

C *e* is vertical

D *d* is horizontal

E *a* and *b* are parallel

10

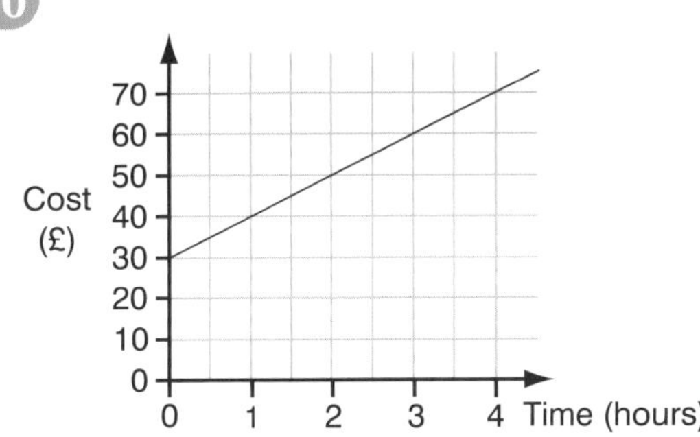

How much does Ben charge for a plumbing job lasting 4 hours?

______

Time for a break! Go to Puzzle Page 45

Total

Test 25: **Mixed**

Test time: 0 5 10 minutes

1

Which number completes the list in order of size?

0.038, ..., 0.042

Circle the answer.

0.0379 0.4 0.04 0.004 0.39

2

A submarine descends from sea level (0 m) to a depth of 150 m.

It then rises 76 m.

How far is it below sea level now?

_______ m below sea level.

3

Which of these makes a word when rotated through 180°?

Circle the answer.

NOOS ENO ONNS ENNA OOB

4

Which answer is different from the others?

Circle the answer.

A 0.1 of 20 **B** 10% of 20 **C** $\frac{1}{10}$ of 20

D 20% of 10 **E** 0.01 of 20

5

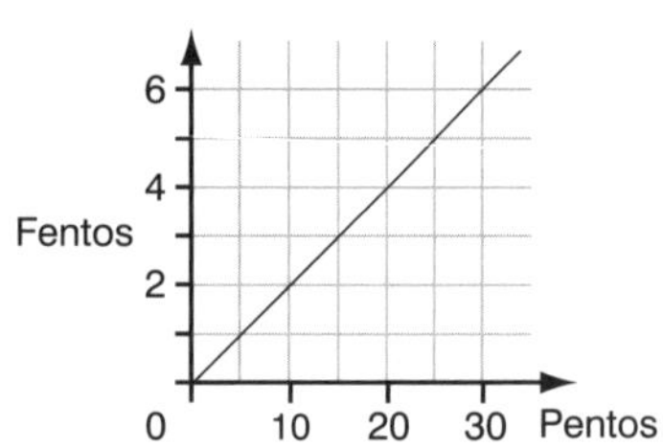

How many Fentos are equivalent to 25 Pentos?

_______ Fentos

6

Complete the function machine.

_____ → ×2 → −1 → **89**

7

This is a net of an open cube.

It is folded to make an open box.

What is the volume of the box?

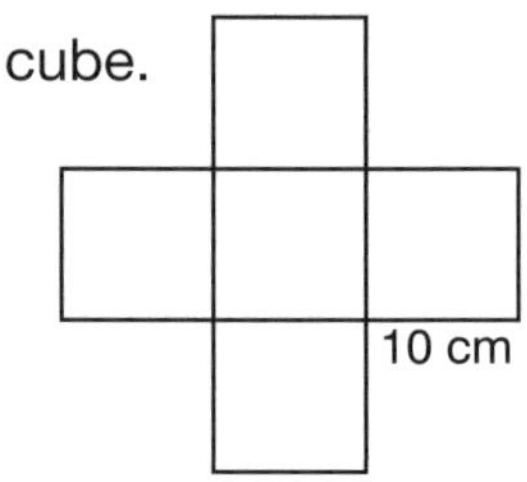

__________ cm^3

8

Which two of these polygons have diagonals that cross at right angles?

Circle the answers.

A Trapezium **B** Square

C Rhombus **D** Regular pentagon

E Rectangle

9

Which is the first number greater than 100 that is divisible by both 3 and 6?

____

10

Jake is driving at a speed of 64 kmh or 40 mph.

Lee is cycling at a speed of 32 kmh or 20 mph.

Roger is travelling on a motorbike at a speed of 96 kmh.

What is his speed in mph?

_______ mph

Total

TEST 26: Mixed

Test time: 0 5 10 minutes

1

What number does the arrow point to?

______

2

Complete the function machine.

72 → ÷6 → ×15 → ______

3

Which of the following will hold about 5 ml?
Circle the answer.

A a teaspoon **B** a swimming pool
C a mug **D** a bucket
E a reservoir

4

The area of a rectangle is 30 cm^2.
Which could be the perimeter of the rectangle?
Circle the answer.

A 6 cm **B** 9 cm **C** 12 cm
D 22 cm **E** 28 cm

5

What is the difference between 9°C and −2°C?

______ °C

6 5.9945

Write this number to two decimal places.

______

7

A school sells 700 concert tickets for £3.99 each.
How much money did they raise?

______

8

Sue thinks of a positive number, multiplies it by itself and then halves the answer.
The number she ends up with is 18.
What was her original number?

______

9

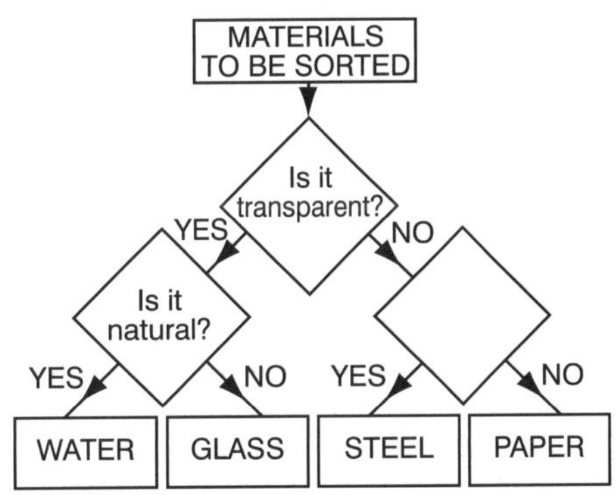

What is missing from the decision tree?
Circle the answer.

A IT IS WEAK. **B** IT IS STRONG.
C IT IS TRANSPARENT. **D** Is it strong?
E Is it opaque?

10

In a maths test Andy gets 30 out of the 35 questions correct.
What proportion has he got right?
Circle the answer.

$\frac{5}{7}$ $\frac{6}{7}$ $\frac{3}{5}$ $\frac{3}{4}$ $\frac{5}{6}$

Total

Test 27: **Mixed**

Test time: 0 5 10 minutes

1

A map has a scale of 1 : 25 000.

What does 4 cm on the map represent in actual distance?

Circle the answer.

A 25 m

B 25 km

C 100 m

D 100 km

E 1 km

2

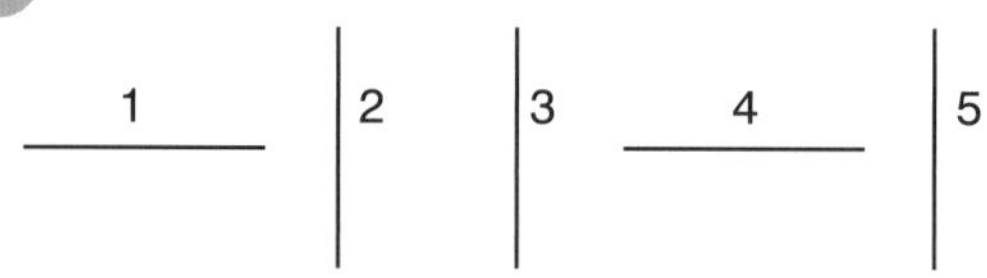

Which of the statements is incorrect?

Circle the answer.

A 2, 3 and 5 are parallel

B 2, 3 and 5 are vertical

C 1 and 4 are parallel

D 1 is perpendicular to 2

E 5 is horizontal

3

The time in Thornsburg is 6 hours ahead of London.

The time in London is 8.27 pm.

What is the time in Thornsburg?

Circle the answer.

A 2.27 pm

B 14.27

C 02.27 pm

D 02.27

E 14.27 am

4

Guide the robot through the grid without hitting any animals.

He can only move FORWARD, TURN LEFT 90° and TURN RIGHT 90°.

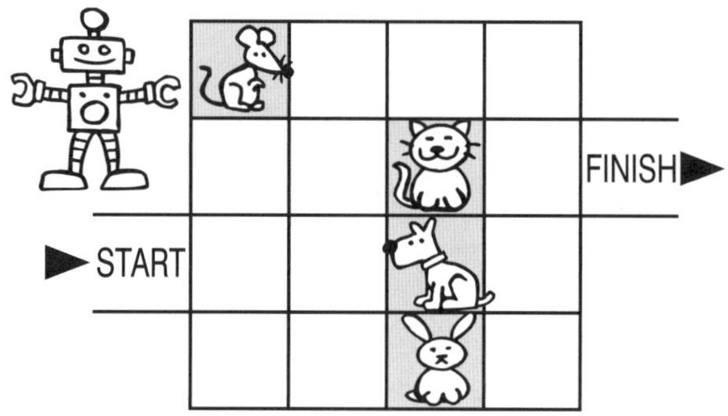

Circle the correct instructions.

A FORWARD 4, TURN LEFT 90°, FORWARD 1, TURN RIGHT 90°, FORWARD 1

B FORWARD 1, TURN LEFT 90°, FORWARD 2, TURN RIGHT 90°, FORWARD 2, TURN RIGHT 90°, FORWARD 1, TURN LEFT 90°, FORWARD 2

C FORWARD 1, TURN LEFT 90°, FORWARD 2, TURN RIGHT 90°, FORWARD 2, TURN RIGHT 90°, FORWARD 2, TURN LEFT 90°, FORWARD 1

D FORWARD 2, TURN LEFT 90°, FORWARD 2, TURN RIGHT 90°, FORWARD 2, TURN RIGHT 90°, FORWARD 1, TURN LEFT 90°, FORWARD 1

E FORWARD 2, TURN LEFT 90°, FORWARD 2, TURN RIGHT 90°, FORWARD 2, TURN RIGHT 90°, FORWARD 2, TURN LEFT 90°, FORWARD 1

5

An ammeter shows current of 4 amps (A).

There are 1000 mA to 1 amp.

The current drops by 500 mA.

What reading does the ammeter now show?

_______ A

6

Convert the list below to fractions and find the smallest fraction.

Circle the answer.

A 30 minutes as a fraction of 2 hours

B 20 minutes as a fraction of 3 hours

C 15 minutes as a fraction of 2 hours

D 40 minutes as a fraction of 1 hour

E 10 minutes as a fraction of 1 hour

7

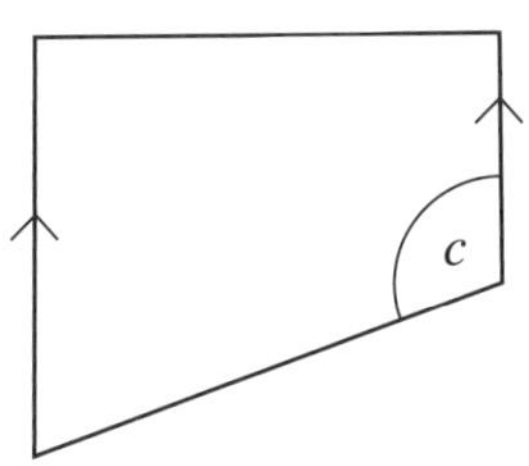

What is the approximate size of the angle marked c in the trapezium?

Circle the answer.

A 150°

B 110°

C 90°

D 60°

E 300°

8

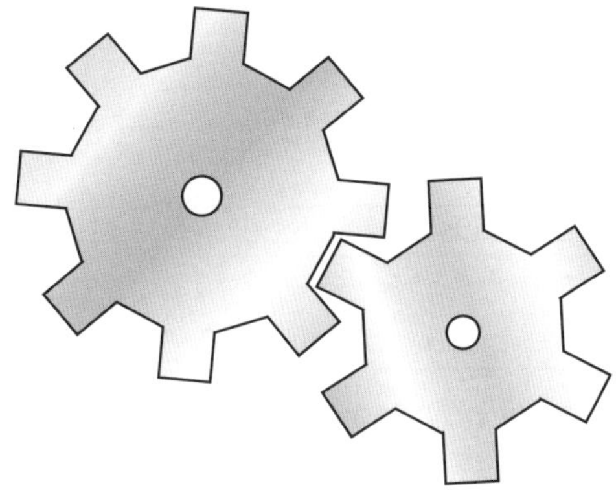

The cog with 8 grooves makes 12 complete revolutions.

How many complete revolutions will the cog with 6 grooves have made?

____

9

Complete the function machine.

27 → ×7 → ÷3 → _______

10

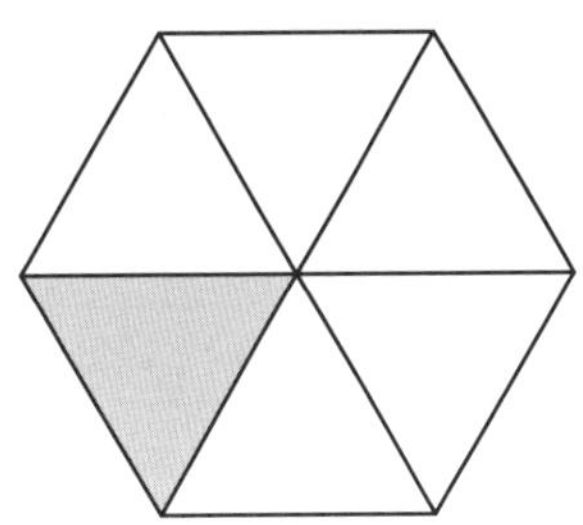

How many more triangles need to be shaded so 50% of the hexagon is shaded?

Circle the answer.

1 2 3 4 5

Total

TEST 28: **Mixed**

1

John collected the following data from 100 children.

	Drum	Recorder	Guitar
Boys	3	?	12
Girls	23	18	18

How many boys gave the recorder as their favourite instrument?

____

2

Lia thinks of a positive number.

She multiplies it by itself and gets 144.

What was the number she started with?

____

3

14 000 people each pay £25 for a concert ticket.

How much money is raised?

£________

4

What is the missing number?

135	148	109
122	?	148
109	122	135

____

5

Out of 600 people interviewed, 378 liked watching soap operas.

What percentage of people surveyed liked watching soap operas?

____

6

Pat collected the following data from 100 pupils.

	Tennis	Judo	Ballet
Boys	13	1	18
Girls	54	3	?

How many girls gave ballet as their favourite activity?

____

7

This is a net of an open cuboid.

It is then folded to make an open box.

What is the volume of the box?

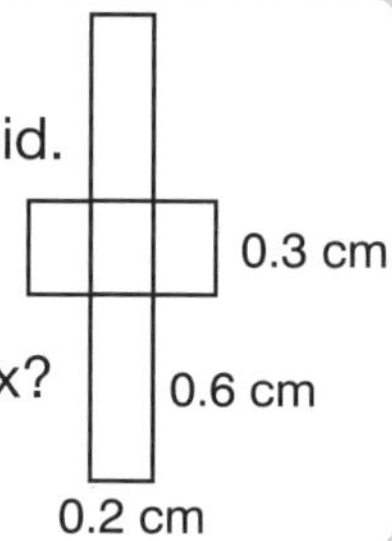

__________ cm^3

8

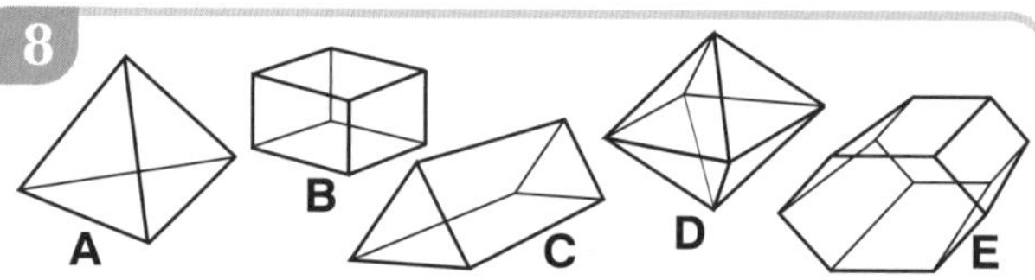

Which shape has 3 edges less than shape D?

____

9

Lara usually buys 150 g bags of crisps.

She sees a bag which is 30% larger.

What is the weight of the large bag?

________ g

10

If p is $\frac{3}{4}$ of q, what is $3q$?

____

Total

TEST 29: **Mixed**

Test time: 0 5 10 minutes

1

The table below shows the atmospheric temperature at different altitudes.

Altitude above sea level (ft)	Temperature (°C)
1 000	10
2 000	8
5 000	2
15 000	−8
20 000	−23
50 000	−67

Which altitude is the coldest?

__________ ft

2

What is the size of the angle marked b in the isosceles triangle?

Circle the answer.

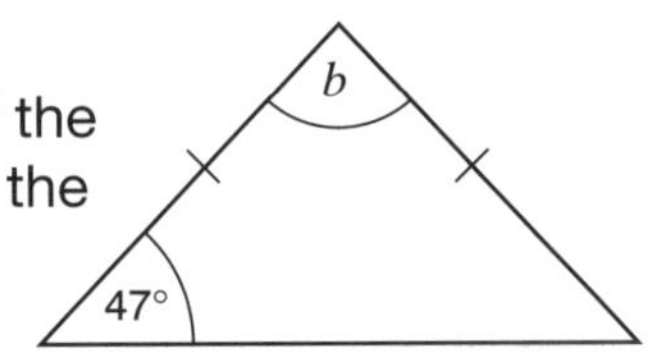

A 266° **B** 86° **C** 96° **D** 47° **E** 153°

3

Mia travels 40 miles before she has a rest.

Her total journey is 50 miles.

What fraction of her journey has she completed?

____

4

Find the range for the hours of sunshine shown in the table.

Month	May	June	July	Aug	Sep
Hours	172	171	189	197	186

Circle the answer.

A 171 **B** 26 **C** 184 **D** 5 **E** 25

5

Kim is ordering some stationery.

She orders x boxes of pencils each containing 50 pencils.

She orders y boxes of pens each containing 20 pens.

How many items does she order?

Leave your answer in terms of x and y.

____

6

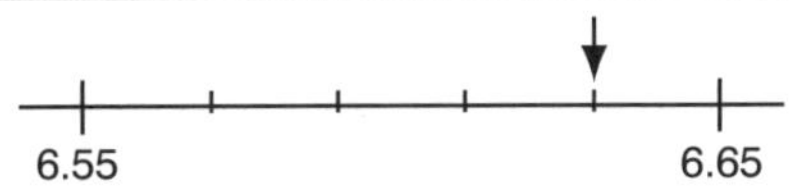

What number does the arrow point to?

____

7

Headache tablets are sold in packets of 18.

How many complete packets can be made from 293 tablets?

____

8

Which ratio is NOT the same as the ratio 12 : 60? Circle the letter.

A 6 : 30 **B** 2 : 10 **C** 1 : 5

D 5 : 1 **E** 24 : 120

9 1 8 9 15 16

Which is **neither** a square number **nor** a cube number? Circle the answer.

10

The Hundred Years War began in 1337 and finished in 1453. How long did it last?

____

Total

TEST 30: **Mixed**

Test time: 0 5 10 minutes

1

Stu was y years old 13 years ago.
How old will he be in 2 years time?
Leave your answer in terms of y.

____

2

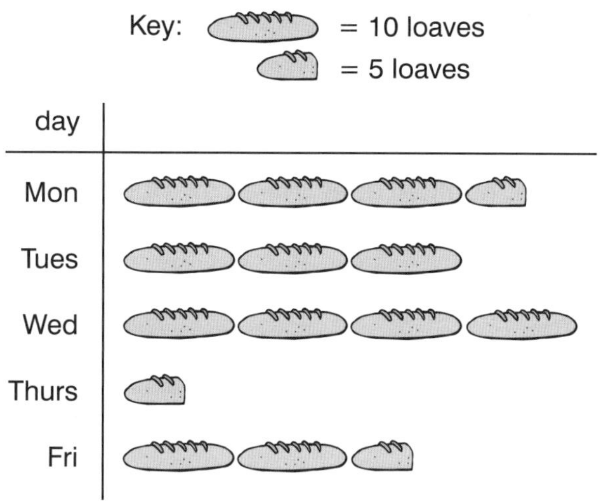

The shop almost ran out of stock one day and had to shut early.
Which day do you think this occurred?

____

3

There are 360 books in the school library.
$\frac{1}{5}$ of the books are fiction.
$\frac{2}{5}$ of the books are non-fiction.
The rest are reference books.
How many reference books are in the library?

____

4

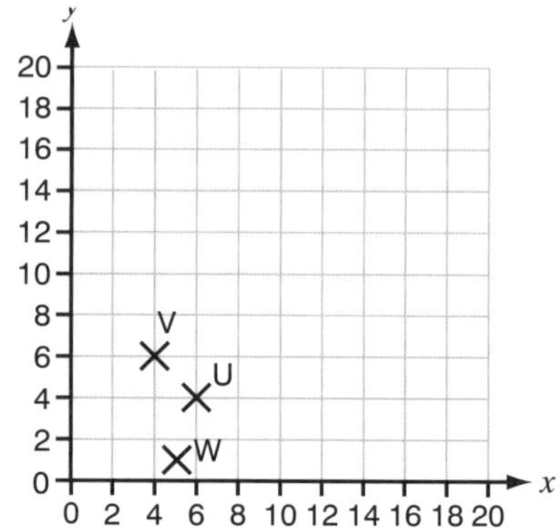

Look at the grid shown.
What are the coordinates of the points U, V and W?
Circle the answer.

A U(6, 4) V(4, 6) W(5, 1)
B U(4, 6) V(6, 4) W(1, 5)
C U(3, 2) V(2, 3) W(2.5, 0.5)
D U(6, 4) V(4, 6) W(4, 2)
E U(6, 4) V(4, 6) W(6, 2)

5

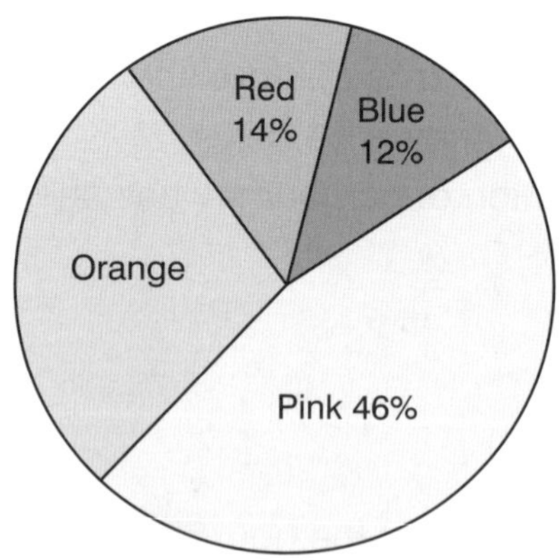

750 people were asked their favourite colour.
The results are displayed in the pie chart.
How many people liked orange?

____

6

Year	Won	Drawn	Lost
2002	4	4	12
2003	6	6	8
2004	5	8	7

How many matches in total did the table tennis team not win?

____

7

	18	
58		20
19		?

When every space is filled in, each row and each column adds up to 117.

Which number should replace the question mark?

____

8

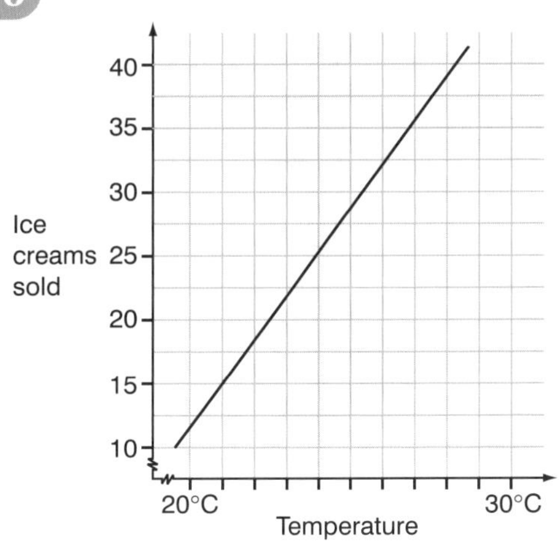

The graph shows the number of ice creams sold depending on the temperature of the day. How many ice creams were sold when the temperature was 21°C?

____

9

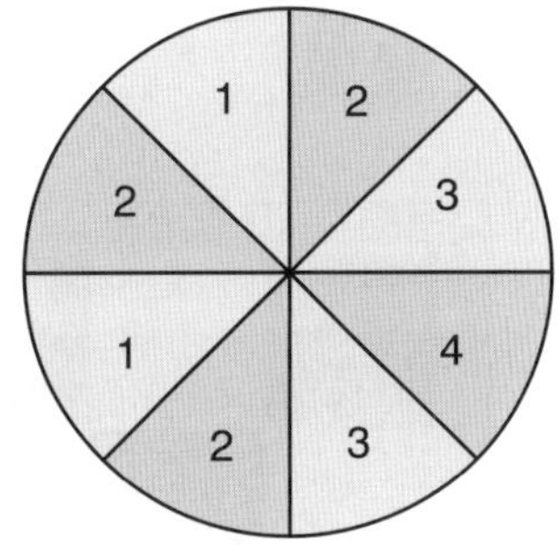

A game is shown above.

Players have to throw a dart at the board and whichever sector (wedge) the dart lands in is their score for that round.

The darts can not land on the borders.

All the throws of the darts are fair.

What is the probability of obtaining an odd number on the throw of the dart?

____

10

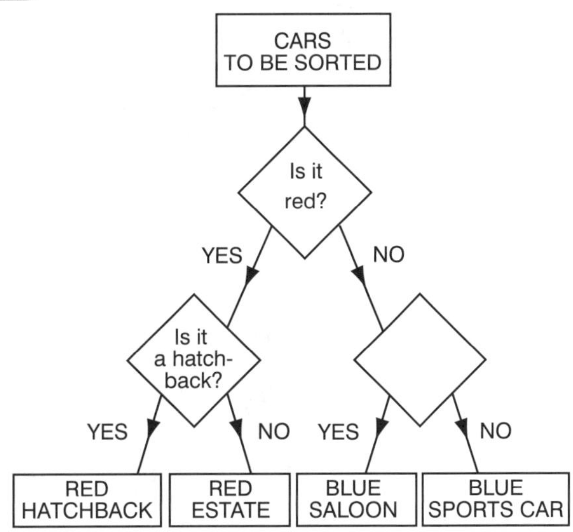

What is missing from the decision tree?

Circle the answer.

A Is it a sports car?

B IT IS A SPORTS CAR.

C Is it blue?

D IT IS BLUE.

E Is it a saloon?

Time for a break! Go to Puzzle Page 46

Total

Puzzle 1

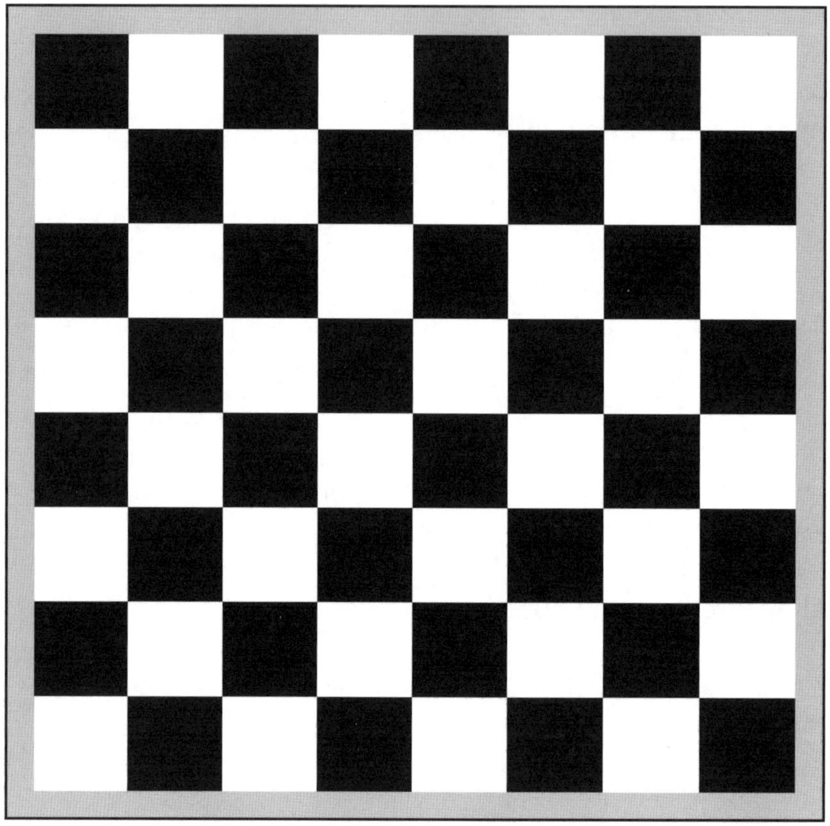

How many squares are on a chessboard? ______________

Clues:

a How many different sized squares can you find? ______________

b How many of the smallest squares can you find? ______________

c How many of the other sizes of squares can you find? ______________

Puzzle 2

An office block has thirty offices numbered 1, 2, 3, up to 30.

Thirty caretakers work at the offices and they all flick the light switches before they leave at the end of the day.

They don't care whether the lights are on or off.
If the lights are on, they switch them off and if the lights are off they switch them on!

The first caretaker who leaves, switches every light off.

The second caretaker who leaves, flicks every second switch starting with office number two.

The third caretaker who leaves, flicks every third switch starting with office number three.

The fourth caretaker who leaves, flicks every fourth switch starting with office number four.

This continues until the thirtieth caretaker leaves and only flicks the switch in office number thirty.

a Which offices are left with the lights off? ______________________

b What is special about these office numbers? ______________________

Puzzle 3

Complete the grid by answering the questions below.

■	1	2	■	3	4	■
5	■	6	7	■	8	9
10	11	■	12	13	■	
■	14	15	■	16	17	■
18	■	19	20	■	21	22
23	24	■	25	26	■	
■	27		■	28		■

Across

1 a dozen
3 half of one hundred and ten
6 a square number
8 three cubed
10 a multiple of thirteen
12 five squared plus six squared
14 six squared plus seven squared plus two
16 102 – 11
19 37 + 6
21 seven squared
23 two squared plus five squared
25 100 – 17
27 60 + 7
28 51 – 3

Down

2 a prime number
4 23 + 29
5 seven eights
7 a multiple of eleven
9 a number divisible by seven and eleven
11 79 – 21
13 a factor of nineteen
15 a multiple of thirty-seven
17 the number of pounds in a stone
18 double twenty-one
20 a multiple of nineteen
22 a multiple of twenty-three
24 two squared less than ten squared
26 divisible by seventeen

Puzzle 4

The numbers shown are the totals of the four numbers in that row or column.

27
26

	20		

Find the remaining totals and write them in the empty total boxes.

Puzzle 5

Five boxes each hold some one kilogram weights.
No two boxes weigh the same.

Their total weight is 31 kilograms.

It is possible to make any weight up to 31 kilograms using one or more boxes.

How much does each box weigh?

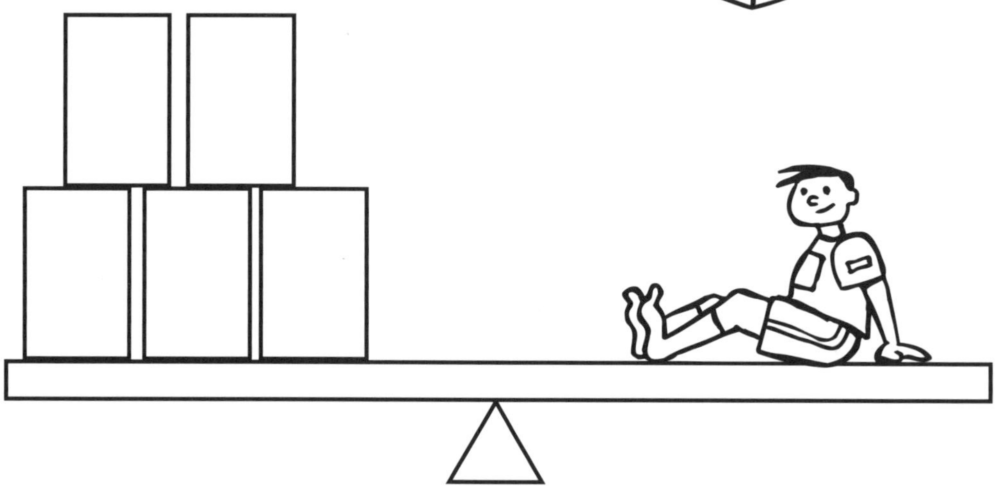

_______ _______ _______ _______ _______

Progress Grid

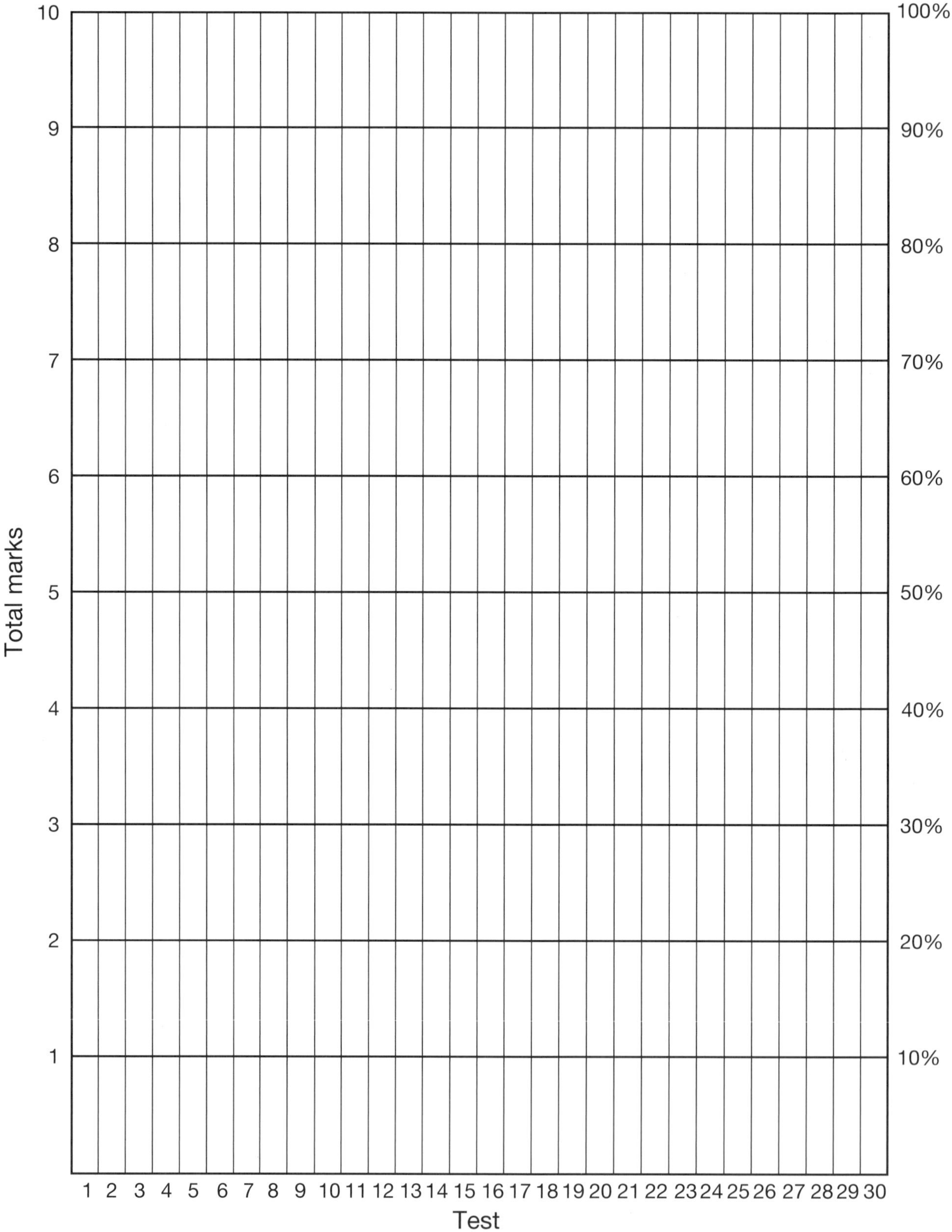